Workshop on Text and Citation Analysis for Scholarly Digital Libraries 2009

(NLPIR4DL 2009)

Held at ACL-IJCNLP 2009

Singapore
7 August 2009

ISBN: 978-1-61738-458-5

Printed from e-media with permission by:

Curran Associates, Inc.
57 Morehouse Lane
Red Hook, NY 12571

Printed by Curran Associates, Inc. (2010)

For permission requests, please contact the Association for Computational Linguistics at the address below.

Association for Computational Linguistics
209 N. Eighth Street
Stroudsburg, Pennsylvania 18360

Phone: 1-570-476-8006
Fax: 1-570-476-0860

acl@aclweb.org

Additional copies of this publication are available from:

Curran Associates, Inc.
57 Morehouse Lane
Red Hook, NY 12571 USA
Phone: 845-758-0400
Fax: 845-758-2634
Email: curran@proceedings.com
Web: www.proceedings.com

Introduction

In recent years, interest in scholarly publications in electronic forms has boomed, and several large-scale electronic digital libraries and citation indices are now used everyday by researchers.

The fact that formal citation metrics have become an increasingly large factor in decision-making by universities and funding bodies worldwide makes the need for research in such topics and for better methods for measuring the impact of work more pressing.

Current digital libraries collect and allow access to digital papers and their metadata (including citations), but largely do not attempt to analyze the items they collect.

The goal of this workshop is to investigate how developments in natural language processing and information retrieval techniques can advance the state-of-the-art in scholarly document understanding, analysis and retrieval.

We were amazed by the number of high-quality papers we received to this inaugural workshop, and by the innovativeness of the research that is done in this area. The contributions split into various areas, and we will here give a quick overview of what these are.

Full document text analysis can help design information access, namely automatic summarization and sentiment detection methods, automated recommendation and reviewing systems, and may provide data for visualizing scientific trends and bibliometrics. *Kaplan et al.*'s paper studies the interaction of citation contexts and co-reference for scientific summarization. Discourse analysis also is the focus of *Merity et al*'s paper which presents an ME-based approach to Argumentative Zoning, and of *Sándor and Vorndran*'s reviewing support system.

We are particularly proud to have two user studies on navigation and search at this workshop, because better systems for information access require such studies as a starting point. *Hearst and Stoica* present a user study and prototype system for faceted navigation in scholarly digital libraries, whereas the study by *Wan et al.* is collecting the browsing-specific information needs by medical searchers, in particular those that could be satisfied by citations and their contexts.

As far as improvement of academic search itself is concerned, the topic of *Shi et al.*'s paper is improved anchor text extraction.

Citation analysis takes this a step further, adding scientific social network analysis as another strand of evidence to enhance solutions to the above challenges. Web based digital libraries add download counts and Web 2.0 information such as tagging.

This workshop contains three papers on citation support in the strictest sense, namely *Hong et al.*, with a fast and lightweight reference string extractor, and *Romanello et al.*, with a recogniser for canonical references, and also a paper on the extraction of researcher affiliation, namely *Nagy et al.*

Aside from researchers, this workshop hopes to interest other stakeholders, namely implementers, publishers and policymakers. For instance, *Nanba and Takezawa*'s research into the Patent Classification Support goes in this direction. Even within computer science, many different scholarly sites exist – ACM Portal, IEEE Xplore, Google Scholar, PSU's CiteSeerX, MSRA's Libra, Tsinghua's

ArnetMiner, Trier's DBLP, UMass' Rexa, Hiroshima's PRESRI – and with this workshop we hope to bring a number of these contributers together. *Radev et al.*'s work on the ACL Anthology Network Corpus reports one such invaluable resource.

Today's publishers continue to seek new ways to be relevant to their consumers, in disseminating the right published works to their audience. Dr. Rick Lee, who is the Director for MIS and Electronic Publishing at the World Scientific Publishing Company, is our invited speaker and will talk about his company's strategy to serve content to the user in future-proof ways.

All that is left after this brief overview of the work in this workshop is to wish all participants a good and informative day.

The organisers of the first NLPIR4DL workshop,

Simone Teufel
Min-Yen Kan

Organizers:

Min-Yen Kan, National University of Singapore
Simone Teufel, University of Cambridge

Program Committee:

Colin Batchelor, Royal Society of Chemistry
Steven Bird, University of Melbourne and the Linguistic Data Consortium
Shannon Bradshaw, Drew University
Jason S Chang, National Tsing-hua University
Robert Dale, Macquarie University
Bonnie Dorr, University of Maryland
Curtis Dyreson, Utah State University
David Ellis, Facebook
C. Lee Giles, Pennsylvania State University
Dan Jurafsky, Stanford University
Noriko Kando, National Institute of Informatics, Japan
Dongwon Lee, Pennsylvania State University
Elizabeth Liddy, Syracuse University
Andrew McCallum, University of Massachusetts
Qiaozhu Mei, University of Illinois at Urbana-Champaign
Hidetsugu Nanba, Hiroshima University
Manabu Okumura, Tokyo Institute of Technology
Dragomir Radev, University of Michigan
Anna Ritchie, University of Cambridge
Mark Sanderson, University of Sheffield
John Swales, University of Michigan
Jie Tang, Tsinghua University
Michael Thelwall, University of Wolverhampton
Bonnie Webber, University of Edinburgh
Howard White, Drexel University

Additional Reviewers:

Johannes Schanda, Sheffield of University

Invited Speaker:

Rick Lee, World Scientific Publishing Company

Table of Contents

Conference Program

Friday, August 7, 2009

9:00 Opening Remarks

9:10–10:00 Invited Talk by Rick Lee of the World Scientific Publishing Company

10:00–10:30 Coffee Break

Session 1: Metadata and Content

10:30–10:55 *Researcher affiliation extraction from homepages*
István Nagy, Richárd Farkas and Márk Jelasity

10:55–11:20 *Anchor Text Extraction for Academic Search*
Shuming Shi, Fei Xing, Mingjie Zhu, Zaiqing Nie and Ji-Rong Wen

11:20–11:45 *Accurate Argumentative Zoning with Maximum Entropy models*
Stephen Merity, Tara Murphy and James R. Curran

11:45–12:10 *Classification of Research Papers into a Patent Classification System Using Two Translation Models*
Hidetsugu Nanba and Toshiyuki Takezawa

12:10–13:50 Lunch Break

Session 2: System Aspects

13:50–14:15 *Detecting key sentences for automatic assistance in peer reviewing research articles in educational sciences*
Ágnes Sándor and Angela Vorndran

14:15–14:40 *Designing a Citation-Sensitive Research Tool: An Initial Study of Browsing-Specific Information Needs*
Stephen Wan, Cécile Paris, Michael Muthukrishna and Robert Dale

14:40–15:05 *The ACL Anthology Network*
Dragomir R. Radev, Pradeep Muthukrishnan and Vahed Qazvinian

15:05–15:30 *NLP Support for Faceted Navigation in Scholarly Collection*
Marti A. Hearst and Emilia Stoica

Friday, August 7, 2009 (continued)

15:30–16:00 Coffee Break

Session 3: Citation Support

16:00–16:25 *FireCite: Lightweight real-time reference string extraction from webpages*
Ching Hoi Andy Hong, Jesse Prabawa Gozali and Min-Yen Kan

16:25–16:50 *Citations in the Digital Library of Classics: Extracting Canonical References by Using Conditional Random Fields*
Matteo Romanello, Federico Boschetti and Gregory Crane

16:50–17:15 *Automatic Extraction of Citation Contexts for Research Paper Summarization: A Coreference-chain based Approach*
Dain Kaplan, Ryu Iida and Takenobu Tokunaga

17:15–18:00 Informal Demonstration Sessions - Wrap up

Researcher affiliation extraction from homepages

István Nagy[1], **Richárd Farkas**[1,2], **Márk Jelasity**[2]
Nagy.Istvan@gmail.com, {rfarkas,jelasity}@inf.u-szeged.hu
[1] University of Szeged, Department of Informatics
Árpad tér 2., H-6720 Szeged, Hungary
[2] Hungarian Academy of Sciences, Research Group on Artificial Intelligence
Aradi vértanuk tere 1., H-6720 Szeged, Hungary

Abstract

Our paper discusses the potential use of Web Content Mining techniques for gathering scientific social information from the homepages of researchers. We will introduce our system which seeks [*affiliation, position, start year, end year*] information tuples on these homepages along with preliminary experimental results. We believe that the lessons learnt from these experiments may be useful for further scientific social web mining.

1 Introduction

Scientific social network analysis (Yang et al., 2009; Said et al., 2008) seeks to discover global patterns in the network of researchers working in a particular field. Common approaches uses bibliographic/scholarly data as the basis for this analysis. In this paper, we will discuss the potential of exploiting other resources as an information source, such as the homepages of researchers. The homepage of a researcher contains several useful pieces of scientific social information like the name of their supervisor, affiliations, academic ranking and so on.

The information on homepages may be present in a structured or natural text form. Here we shall focus on the detection and analysis of full text regions of the homepages as they may contain a huge amount of information while requires more sophisticated analysis than that for structured ones. We will show that this kind of Web-based Relation Extraction requires different techniques than the state-of-the-art seed-based approaches as it has to acquire information from the long-tail of the World Wide Web.

As a case study, we chose one particular scientific social information type and sought to extract information tuples concerning the previous and current *affiliations* of the researcher in question. We defined 'affiliation' as the current and previous physical workplaces and higher educational institutes of the researcher in question. Our aim is to use this kind of information to discover collegial relationships and workplace-changing behaviour which may be complementary to the items of information originating from bibliographic databases.

Based on a manually annotated corpus we carried out several information extraction experiments. The architecture of the complex system and the recognised problems will be discussed in Section 3, while our empirical results will be presented in Section 4. In the last two sections we will briefly discuss our results and then draw our main conclusions.

2 Related work

The relationship to previous studies will be discussed from a scientific social network analysis as an application point of view and from a Web Content Mining point of view as well.

2.1 Researcher affiliation extraction

Scientific social network analysis has become a growing area in recent years ((Yang et al., 2009; Robardet and Fleury, 2009; Said et al., 2008) just to name a few in recent studies). Its goal is to provide a deeper insight into a research field or into the personal connections among fields by analysing relationships among researchers. The existing studies use the co-authorship (e.g. (Newman, 2001; Barabási et al., 2002)) or/and the citation (Goodrum et al., 2001; Teufel et al., 2006) information – generally by constructing a graph with nodes representing researchers – as the basis for their investigations.

Apart from publication-related relationships – which are presented in structured scholarly datasets –, useful scientific social information can

Proceedings of the 2009 Workshop on Text and Citation Analysis for Scholarly Digital Libraries, ACL-IJCNLP 2009, pages 1–9,
Suntec, Singapore, 7 August 2009. ©2009 ACL and AFNLP

be gathered from the WWW. Take, for instance the homepage of a researchers where they summarise their *topic of interest*, list *supervisors* and *students*, *nationality*, *age*, *memberships* and so on. Our goal is to develop an automatic Web Content Mining system which crawls the homepages of researchers and extracts useful social information from them.

A case study will be outlined here, where the previous and current affiliations of the researcher in question were gathered automatically. Having a list of normalised *affiliations* for each researcher of a field (i) we ought to be able to discover collegial relationships (whether they worked with the same group at the same time) which may differ from the co-authorship relation and (ii) we hope to be able to answer questions like *'Do American or European researchers change their workplace more often?'*.

2.2 Information extraction from homepages

From a technology point of view our procedure is a Web Content Mining tool, but it differs from the popular techniques used nowadays. The aim of Web Content Mining (Liu and Chen-Chuan-Chang, 2004) is to extract useful information from the natural language-written parts of websites.

The first attempts on Web Content Mining began with the Internet around 1998-'99 (Adelberg, 1998; Califf and Mooney, 1999; Freitag, 1998; Kosala and Blockeel, 2000). They were expert systems with hand-crafted rules or induced rules used in a supervised manner and based on labeled corpora.

The next generation of approaches on the other hand work in weakly-supervised settings (Etzioni et al., 2005; Sekine, 2006; Bellare et al., 2007). Here, the input is a seed list of target information pairs and the goal is to gather a set of pairs which are related to each other in the same manner as the seed pairs. These pairs may contain related entities (for example, *country - capital city* in (Etzioni et al., 2005) and celebrity partnerships in (Cheng et al., 2009)) or form an entity-attribute pair (like *Nobel Prize recipient - year* in (Feiyu Xu, 2007)) or may be concerned with retrieving all available attributes for entities (Bellare et al., 2007; Paşca, 2009). These systems generally download web pages which contain the seed pairs then learn syntactical/semantical rules from the sentences of the pairs (they generally use the positive instances for one case as negative instances for another case). According to these patterns, they can download a new set of web pages and parse them to acquire new pairs.

These seed-based systems exploit the redundancy of the WWW. They are based on the hypothesis that important information can be found at several places and in several forms on the Web, hence a few accurate rules can be used to collect the required lists. Their goal is to find and recognise (at least) one occurrence of the target information and not to find their every occurrence on the Web. But this is not the case in our scenario. Several pieces of social information for the researchers are available just on their homepages (or nowhere). Thus here we must capture each mention of the information. The weakly-supervised (redundancy-based) systems can build on high-precision and lower recall information extraction, while we have to have target a perfect recall. For the evaluation of such a system we constructed a manually annotated corpus of researchers' homepages. This corpus was also used as a training corpus for the preliminary information extraction experiments described in this paper.

3 The architecture of the system

The general task of our system is to gather scientific social information from the homepages of researchers. In the use case presented in this paper, the input is a set of researchers' names who work in a particular research field (later on, this list can be automatically gathered, for example, from a call for papers) and the output is a list of affiliations for each researcher. Here the affiliation is a tuple of *affiliation*, *position type* and *start/end dates*. We think that the lessons learnt from affiliation extraction will be useful for the development of a general social information extraction system.

The system has to solve several subproblems which will be described in the following subsections.

3.1 Locating the homepage of the researcher

Homepage candidates can be efficiently found by using *web search engine* queries for the given name. In our case study the homepage of the researcher (when it existed) were among the top 10 responses of the Google API[1] in each case. However, selecting the correct homepage from the top 10 responses is a harder task. Among

[1] http://code.google.com/apis/

these sites there are (i) publication-related ones (books/articles written by the researchers, call for papers), sites of the institute/group associated with the researcher and (ii) homepages of people sharing the same name.

In our preliminary experiments, we ignored these two basic problems and automatically parsed each website. However in the future we plan to develop a two-stage approach to solve them. In the first stage a general homepage detection model – a binary classification problem with classes `homepage/non-homepage` – will be applied. In the second stage we will attempt to automatically extract textual clues for the relations among the researchers (e.g. the particular field they work in) from the homepage candidates and utilise these cues for name disambiguation along with other biographical cues. For a survey of state-of-the-art name disambiguation, see (Artiles et al., 2009).

3.2 Locating the relevant parts of the site

The URL got from the search engine usually points to the main page of the homepage site. An ideal system should automatically find every page which might contain scientific social information like *Curriculum Vitae*, *Research interests*, *Projects* etc. This can be done by analysing the text of the links or even the linked page. In our case study we simply parsed the pages to a depth of 1 (i.e. the main page and each page which was linked from it).

The located web pages usually have their content arranged in sections. The first step of information extraction may be a relevant section selection module. For example, in the affiliation extraction task the *Positions Held* and *Education* type sections are relevant while *Selected Papers* is not. Having several relevant sections with their textual positions, an automatic classification system can filter out a huge number of probably irrelevant sections. In our experiments, we statistically collected a few "relevant keywords" and filtered out sections and paragraphs which did not contain any of these keywords.

3.3 Extracting information tuples

Pieces of scientific social information are usually present on the homepages and in the CVs even in an itemised (structured) form or in a natural language full text form. Information extraction is performed from the structured parts of the documents by automatically constructed rules based on the HTML tags and keywords. This field is called Wrapper Induction (Kushmerick, 2000).

We shall focus on the information extraction from raw texts here because we found that more pages express content in textual form than in a structured one in the researchers' homepages of our case study and this task still has several unsolved problems. We mentioned above that scientific social information extraction has to capture each occurrence of the target information. We manually labeled homepages for the evaluation of these systems. We think that the DOM structure of the homepages (e.g. formatting tags, section headers) could provide useful information, hence the labeling was carried out in their original HTML form (Farkas et al., 2008). In our preliminary experiments we also used this corpus to train classification models (they were evaluated in a one-researcher-leave-out scheme). The purpose of these supervised experiments was to gain an insight into the nature of the problem, but we suggest that a real-world system for this task should work in a weakly-supervised setting.

3.4 Normalisation

The output of the extraction phase outlined above is a list of *affiliation*s for each researcher in the form that occurred in the documents. However, for scientific social network analysis, several normalisation steps should be performed. For example, for collegial relationship extraction, along with the matching of various transliteration of research groups (like *Massachusetts Institute of Technology* and *MIT AI Lab*), we have to identify the appropriate institutional level where two researchers probably still have a personal contact as well.

4 Experiments

Now we will present the affiliation corpus which was constructed manually for evaluation purposes along with several preliminary experiments on affiliation extraction.

4.1 The affiliation corpus

We manually constructed a web page corpus containing HTML documents annotated for publicly available information about researchers. We downloaded 455 sites, 5282 pages for 89 researchers (who form the Programme Committee of the SASO07 conference[2]), and two indepen-

[2]http://projects.csail.mit.edu/saso2007/tmc.html

dent annotators carried out their manual labeling in the original (HTML) format of the web pages, following an annotation guideline (Farkas et al., 2008). All the labels that were judged inconsistent were collected together from the corpus for a review by the two annotators and the chief annotator. We defined a three-level deep annotation hierarchy with 44 classes (labels). The wide range of the labels and the inter-annotator agreement both suggest that the automatic reproduction of this full labelling is a hard task.

We selected one particular information class, namely *affiliation* from our class hierarchy for our case study. We defined 'affiliation' as the current and previous physical workplaces and higher educational institutes of the researcher in question as we would like to use this kind of information to discover collegial relationships and workplace-changing behaviour. Here institutes related to review activities, awards, or memberships are not regarded as affiliations. We call `position` the tuple of `<affiliation, position_types, years>`, as for example in <*National Department of Computer Science and Operational Research at the University of Montreal, adjunct Professor*, {*1995*, *2002*}>[3]. Among the four slots just the `affiliation` slot is mandatory (it is the head) as the others are usually missing in real homepages.

The problem of finding the relevant pages of a homepage site originating from a seed URL was not addressed in this study. We found that pages holding affiliation information was the one retrieved by Google in 135 cases and directly linked to the main page in 50 cases. We found affiliation information for all of the 89 researchers of our case study in the depth of 1, but we did not check whether deeper crawling could have yielded new information.

The affiliation information (like every piece of scientific social information) can be present on web pages in an itemised or natural text format. We manually investigated our corpus and found that the 47% of the pages contained affiliation information exclusively in a textual form, 24% exclusively in an itemised form and 29% were hybrid. Information extraction from these two formats requires different methods. We decided to address the problem of affiliation extraction just by using the raw text parts of the homepages.

We partitioned each downloaded page at HTML breaking tags and kept the parts (paragraphs) which were regarded as "raw text". Here we used the following rule: *a textual paragraph has to be longer than 40 characters and contain at least one verb*. Certainly this rule is far from perfect (paragraphs describing publication and longer items of lists are still present), but it seems to be a reasonable one as it extracts paragraphs even from 'hybrid' pages. We found 86,735 paragraphs in the 5282 downloaded pages and used them in experiments in a raw `txt` format (HTML tags were removed).

Table 4.1 summarises the size-related figures for the part of this textual corpus which contains affiliation information (these paragraphs contain manually labeled information). The corpus is freely available for non-commercial use[4].

# researchers	59
# pages	103
# paragraph	151
# sentences	181
# `affiliation`	374
# `position_type`	326
# `year`	212

Table 1: The size of the textual corpus which contains affiliation information.

4.2 The multi-stage model of relation extraction

Our relation extraction system follows the architecture described in the previous section. We focus on the *relevant part location* and *information extraction* steps in this study. We applied simple rules to recognise the relevant parts of the homepages. We extract textual paragraphs as described above and then filter out probably irrelevant ones (Section 4.3).

Preliminary supervised information extraction experiments were carried out in our case study in order to get an insight into the special nature of the problem. We used a one-researcher-leave-out evaluation setting (i.e. the train sets consisted of the paragraphs of 88 researchers and the test sets concerned 1 researcher), thus we avoided the situations where a training set contained possibly re-

[3]the example is extracted from http://bcr2.uwaterloo.ca/~rboutaba/biography2.htm

[4]www.inf.u-szeged.hu/rgai/homepagecorpus

dundant information about the subject of the test texts.

A two-stage information extraction system was applied here. In the first phase, a model should recognise each possible slot/entities of the target information tuples (Section 4.4). Then the tuples have to be filled, i.e. the roles have to be assigned and irrelevant entities should be ignored (Section 4.5).

4.3 Paragraph filtering

Because just a small portion of extracted textual paragraphs contained affiliation information, we carried out experiments on filtering out probably irrelevant paragraphs.

Our filtering method exploited the paragraphs containing `position` (positive paragraphs). We calculated the $P(word|positive)$ conditional probabilities and the best words based on this measure (e.g. *university*, *institute* and *professor*) then formed the so-called positive wordset. The paragraphs which did not contain any word from the positive wordset were removed. Note that standard positive and negative sample-based classification is not applicable here as the non-positive paragraphs may contain these indicative words, but in an irrelevant context or with a connection to people outside of our scope of interest. Our 1-DNF hypothesis described above uses just positive examples and it was inspired by (Yu et al., 2002).

After performing this procedure we kept 14,686 paragraphs (from the full set of 86,735), but we did not leave out any annotated text. Hence the information extraction module could then work with a smaller and less noisy dataset.

4.4 Detecting possible slots

We investigated a Named Entity Recognition (NER) tool for detecting possible actors of a `position` tuple. But note that this task is not a classical NER problem because our goal here is to recognise just those entities which may play a role in a `position` event. For example there were many `year` tokens in the text – having the same orthographic properties – but only a few were related to affiliation information. The contexts of the tokens should play an important role in this kind of an NER targeting of very narrow semantic NE classes.

For training and evaluating the NER systems, we used each 151 paragraphs containing at least one manually labeled `position` along with 200 other manually selected paragraphs which do not contain any labeled `position`. We decided to use just this 151+200 paragraphs instead of the full set of 86,735 paragraphs for CPU time reasons. Manual selection – instead of random sampling – was required as there were several paragraphs which contained affiliation information unrelated to the researcher in question, thus introducing noise. In our multi-stage architecture, the NER model trained on this reduced document set was than predicated for the full set of paragraphs and false positives (note that the paragraphs outside the NER-train do not contain any gold-standard annotation) has to be eliminated.

We employed the Condition Random Fields (Lafferty et al., 2001) (implementation MALLET (McCallum, 2002)) for our NER experiments. The feature set employed was developed for general NER and includes the following categories (Szarvas et al., 2006):

orthographical features: capitalisation, word length, bit information about the word form (contains a digit or not, has uppercase character inside the word, and so on), character level bi/trigrams,

dictionaries of first names, company types, denominators of locations,

frequency information: frequency of the token, the ratio of the token's capitalised and lowercase occurrences, the ratio of capitalised and sentence beginning frequencies of the token which was derived from the Gigaword dataset[5],

contextual information: sentence position, trigger words (the most frequent and unambiguous tokens in a window around the NEs) from the train text, the word between quotes, and so on.

This basic set was extended by two domain-specific gazetteers, namely a list of *university names* and *position types*. We should add that a domain-specific exception list (containing e.g. *Dr.*, *Ph.D.*) for augmenting a general sentence splitter was employed here.

Table 2 lists the phrase-level $F_{\beta=1}$ results obtained by CRF in the one-researcher-leave-out

[5]Linguistic Data Consortium (LDC), catalogId: LDC2003T05

evaluation scheme, while Table 3 lists the results of a baseline method which labels each member of the university and position type gazetteers and identifies years using regular expressions. This comparison highlights the fact that labeling each occurrences of this easily recognisable classes cannot be applied. It gives an extremely low precision thus contextual information has to be leveraged.

	Precision	Recall	$F_{\beta=1}$
affiliation	66.78	53.28	59.27
position type	87.50	70.22	77.91
year	86.42	69.31	76.92
TOTAL	78.73	62.88	69.92

Table 2: The results achieved by CRF.

	Precision	Recall	$F_{\beta=1}$
affiliation	21.43	9.68	13.33
position type	23.27	66.77	34.51
year	65.77	98.99	79.03
TOTAL	32.16	44.08	37.19

Table 3: NER baseline results.

4.5 The assignment of roles

When we apply the NER module to unknown documents we have to decide whether the recognised entities have any connection with the particular person as downloaded pages often contain information about other researchers (supervisors, students, etc.) as well. The subject of the information is generally expressed by a proper noun at the beginning of the page or paragraph and then anaphoric references are used. We assumed here that each `position` tuple in a paragraph was related to exactly one person and when the subject of the first sentence of the paragraph was a personal pronoun *I*, *she*, *he* then the paragraph belonged to the author of the page.

To automatically find the subject of the paragraphs we tried out two procedures and evaluated them on the predictions of the NER model introduced in the previous subsection. First, we applied a NER trained on the person names of the CoNLL-2003 corpus (Tjong Kim Sang and De Meulder, 2003). The names predicted by this method were then compared to the owner of the homepage using name normalisation techniques. If no name was found by the tagger we regarded the paragraph as belonging to the author. Its errors had two sources; the NER trained on an out-domain corpus made a lot of false negatives and the normalisation method had to deal with incorrect "names" (like *Paul Hunter Curator* as a name phrase) as well.

The second method was simpler. We kept the `position` tuples whose paragraph contained any part of the researcher name or any of the "*I*", "*she*", "*he*" personal pronouns. Its errors came, for instance, from finding the "*Paul*" string for "*Paul Robertson*" in the text snippet "*Paul Berger*".

We applied these two subject detection methods to the predictions of our slot detection NER modul. Table 4 summarises the accuracies of the systems, i.e. whether they made the correct decision on "is this forecasted affiliation corresponds to the researcher in question". The columns of this table shows how many `affiliation` prediction was carried out by the slot detection system, i.e. how many times has to made a decision. "name. det" and "p. pronouns" refer to the two methods, to the name detection-based and to the personal pronoun-matcher ones. We investigated their performance on the paragraphs which contained manually labeled information, on the paragraphs which did contained any but the slot detection module forecasted at least one `affiliation` here and on the union of these sets of paragraphs. The figures of the table shows that the personal pronoun detection approach performs significantly better on the paragraphs which really contains affiliation information. This is due to the fact that this method removes less prediction compared to the name based one and there are just a few forecast which has to be removed on the paragraphs which contain information.

	#pred	name det.	p. pronouns
annotated	165	66.9	87.8
non-ann.	214	71.5	61.2
full set	379	69.4	73.4

Table 4: Accuracies of subject detection methods.

To find relationships among the other types of predicated entities (*affiliation, position type, start year, end year*) we used a very simple heuristic. As the `affiliation` slot is the head of the tuple we simply assigned every other detected entity to the nearest `affiliation` and regarded the earlier preidcated `year` token as the `start year`.

This method made the correct decision in the 91.3% and 71.8% of the cases applied on the gold-standard annotation and the predicated entities, respectively. We should add that using the predicted labels during the evaluation, the false positives of the NER counts automatically an error in relation detection as well.

5 Discussion

The first step of the information extraction system of this case study was the localisation of relevant information. We found that Web search engines are efficient tools for finding homepages. We empirically showed that a very simple crawling (downloading everything to a depth of 1) can be applied, because the irrelevant contents can be removed later. The advantage of focused crawling (i.e. making a decision before downloading a linked page) is that it can avoid the time-consuming analysis of pages. However making the decision of whether the linked document might contain relevant information is a hard task. On the other hand we showed that the requested information is reachable in depth 1 and that a fast string-matching based filtering method can significantly reduce the amount of texts which have to be analysed without losing any information. Moreover, the positive example-based filtering approach can be employed in a seed-driven setting as well.

For the information extraction phase we think that a high-recall system has to be developed. We constructed a corpus with contextual occurrences for evaluation issues. The extraction can be relationship detection-based (e.g. the state-of-the-art seed-driven approaches seek to acquire syntactic/semantic patterns which are typical of the relationship itself) or entity-based (like our method, these approaches first identify possible actors then look for relationships among them). We expect that the latter one is more suitable for high-recall tasks.

The NER system of this case study achieved significantly better results than those for the baseline method. We experimentally showed that it could exploit the contextual information and that the labeled entities were those which were affiliation-related. However, the overall system has to be improved in the future. We manually analysed the errors on a part of the corpus and found a few typical errors were present. Our annotation guide said that the geographical location of the affiliation was a part of the affiliation as it sometimes identifies the department (e.g. *"Hewlett-Packard Labs in Palo Alto"*). This extension of the phrase proved to be difficult because there were several cases with the same orthographic features (e.g. *Ph.D. from MIT in Physics*). The acronyms immediately after the affiliation are a similar case, which we regard as part of the name and it is difficult for the NER to handle (e.g. *Centre for Policy Modelling (CPM)*). As there is no partial credit; an incorrect entity boundary is penalised both as a false positive and as a false negative.

These points also explain the surprisingly low precision of the baseline system as it labeled university names without more detailed identification of the unit (e.g. *Department of Computer Science, [Waterloo University]$_{BASELINE}$*). We should add that these two annotation guidelines are questionable, but we expect that information might get lost without them. Moreover, there is an another reason for the low recall, it is that our human annotators found textual clues for *position types* on verbs as well (e.g. *I lead$_{TYPE}$ the Distributed Systems Group*). The context of these labeled examples are clearly different from that of the usual *position type*.

Comparing the two subject detection methods, we see that the name detection model which learnt on an out-domain corpus made a lot of mistakes, thus the method based on it judged more paragraphs as irrelevant ones. The name detection could be improved by a domain corpus (for example the training corpus did not contain any *Prof. NAME* example) and by applying more sophisticated name normalisation techniques. When we manually analysed the errors of these procedures we found that each false negative of the simpler subject detection method was due to the errors of the textual paragraph identification definition used. There were several itemisations whose header was type of *"Previously I worked for:"* and the textual items themselves did not contain the subject of the affiliation information. The false positives often originated from pages which did not belong to the researcher in question but contained him name (e.g. *I am a Ph.D. Student working under the supervision of Prof. NAME*).

Lastly, an error analysis of the affiliation head seeking heuristic revealed that the 44% of the predicted `position type` and `year` entities's sentences did not contain any `affiliation` prediction. With the gold-standard labeling, there were 6 sentences without `affiliation` labels and only one of them used an anaphoric reference, the others were a consequence of the erroneous automatic sentence splitting of the HTML documents. The prediction of the NER system contained many more sentences without any `affiliation` label. These could be fixed by forcing a second forecast phase to predict `affiliation` in these sentences or by removing these labels in a post-processing step.

The remaining errors of the affiliation head assignment could be avoided just by employing a proper syntactic analyser. The most important linguistic phenomena which should be automatically identify for this problem is enumeration. For instance, we should distinguish between the enumeration and clause splitting roles of 'and' (e.g. *"I'm a senior researcher and leader of the GROUP"* and *"He got his PhD from UNIVERSITY1 in YEAR and has a Masters from UNIVERSITY2"*). This requires a deep syntactic analysis, i.e. the use of a dependency parser which has to make accurate predictions on several certain types of dependencies is probably needed.

6 Conclusions

In this paper we introduced a Web Content Mining system for gathering affiliation information from the homepages of researchers. The affiliation information collected from this source might be of great value for scientific social network analysis.

We discussed the special nature of this task compared to common Web-based relation extraction approaches and identified several subtasks of the system during our preliminary experiments. We argued that the evaluation of this kind of system should be carried out on a manually labeled reference corpus. We introduced simple but effective solutions for the subproblems along with empirical results on a corpus. We achieved reasonable results with an overall phrase-level $F_{\beta=1}$ score of 70% on the possible slot detection and an accuracy of 61% on relation extraction (as an aggregation of the subject detection and the affiliation head selection procedures). However each subproblem requires more sophisticated solutions, which we plan to address in the near future.

Acknowledgments

This work was supported in part by the NKTH grant of the Jedlik Ányos R&D Programme (project codename TEXTREND) of the Hungarian government. The authors would like to thank the annotators of the corpus for their devoted efforts.

References

Brad Adelberg. 1998. Nodose - a tool for semi-automatically extracting structured and semistructured data from text documents. *ACM SIGMOD*, 27(2):283–294.

Javier Artiles, Julio Gonzalo, and Satoshi Sekine. 2009. Weps 2 evaluation campaign: overview of the web people search clustering task. In *2nd Web People Search Evaluation Workshop (WePS 2009), 18th WWW Conference*.

A. L. Barabási, H. Jeong, Z. Néda, E. Ravasz, A. Schubert, and T. Vicsek. 2002. Evolution of the social network of scientific collaborations. *Physica A: Statistical Mechanics and its Applications*, 311(3-4):590 – 614.

Kedar Bellare, Partha Talukdar, Giridhar Kumaran, Fernando Pereira, Mark Liberman, Andrew McCallum, and Mark Dredze. 2007. Lightly-supervised attribute extraction for web search. In *Proceedings of NIPS 2007 Workshop on Machine Learning for Web Search*.

Mary Elaine Califf and Raymond J. Mooney. 1999. Relational learning of pattern-match rules for information extraction. In *Proceedings of the Sixteenth National Conference on Artificial Intelligence*, pages 328–334.

Xiwen Cheng, Peter Adolphs, Feiyu Xu, Hans Uszkoreit, and Hong Li. 2009. Gossip galore – a self-learning agent for exchanging pop trivia. In *Proceedings of the Demonstrations Session at EACL 2009*, pages 13–16, Athens, Greece, April. Association for Computational Linguistics.

Oren Etzioni, Michael Cafarella, Doug Downey, Ana maria Popescu, Tal Shaked, Stephen Soderl, Daniel S. Weld, and Er Yates. 2005. Unsupervised named-entity extraction from the web: An experimental study. *Artificial Intelligence*, 165:91–134.

Richárd Farkas, Róbert Ormándi, Márk Jelasity, and János Csirik. 2008. A manually annotated html corpus for a novel scientific trend analysis. In *Proc. of The Eighth IAPR Workshop on Document Analysis Systems*.

Hong Li Feiyu Xu, Hans Uszkoreit. 2007. A seed-driven bottom-up machine learning framework for extracting relations of various complexity. In *Proceedings of ACL 2007, 45th Annual Meeting of the Association for Computational Linguistics*, Prague, Czech Republic, 6.

Dayne Freitag. 1998. Information extraction from html: Application of a general machine learning approach. In *Proceedings of the Fifteenth National Conference on Artificial Intelligence*, pages 517–523.

A. A Goodrum, K. W McCain, S. Lawrence, and C. L Giles. 2001. Scholarly publishing in the internet age: a citation analysis of computer science literature. *Information Processing and Management*, 37:661–675, September.

Raymond Kosala and Hendrik Blockeel. 2000. Web mining research: A survey. *SIGKDD Explorations*, 2:1–15.

Nicholas Kushmerick. 2000. Wrapper induction: Efficiency and expressiveness. *Artificial Intelligence*, 118:2000.

John Lafferty, Andrew McCallum, and Fernando Pereira. 2001. Conditional random fields: Probabilistic models for segmenting and labeling sequence data. In *Proc. 18th International Conf. on Machine Learning*, pages 282–289. Morgan Kaufmann, San Francisco, CA.

Bing Liu and Kevin Chen-Chuan-Chang. 2004. Editorial: special issue on web content mining. *SIGKDD Explor. Newsl.*, 6(2):1–4.

Andrew Kachites McCallum. 2002. Mallet: A machine learning for language toolkit. http://mallet.cs.umass.edu.

M. E. J. Newman. 2001. The structure of scientific collaboration networks. In *Proceedings National Academy of Sciences USA*, pages 404–418.

Marius Paşca. 2009. Outclassing Wikipedia in open-domain information extraction: Weakly-supervised acquisition of attributes over conceptual hierarchies. In *Proceedings of the 12th Conference of the European Chapter of the ACL (EACL 2009)*, Athens, Greece, March.

Celine Robardet and Eric Fleury. 2009. Communities detection and the analysis of their dynamics in collaborative networks. *Int. J. Web Based Communities*, 5(2):195–211.

Yasmin H. Said, Edward J. Wegman, Walid K. Sharabati, and John T. Rigsby. 2008. Social networks of author-coauthor relationships. *Computational Statistics & Data Analysis*, 52(4):2177–2184.

Satoshi Sekine. 2006. On-demand information extraction. In *Proceedings of the COLING/ACL 2006 Main Conference Poster Sessions*, pages 731–738, Sydney, Australia, July. Association for Computational Linguistics.

György Szarvas, Richárd Farkas, and András Kocsor. 2006. A multilingual named entity recognition system using boosting and c4.5 decision tree learning algorithms. *DS2006, LNAI*, 4265:267–278.

Simone Teufel, Advaith Siddharthan, and Dan Tidhar. 2006. An annotation scheme for citation function. In *Proceedings of the 7th SIGdial Workshop on Discourse and Dialogue*, pages 80–87, Sydney, Australia, July. Association for Computational Linguistics.

Erik F. Tjong Kim Sang and Fien De Meulder. 2003. Introduction to the conll-2003 shared task: Language-independent named entity recognition. In Walter Daelemans and Miles Osborne, editors, *Proceedings of CoNLL-2003*, pages 142–147. Edmonton, Canada.

Y. Yang, C. M. Au Yeung, M. J. Weal, and H. Davis. 2009. The researcher social network: A social network based on metadata of scientific publications.

Hwanjo Yu, Jiawei Han, and Kevin Chen-Chuan Chang. 2002. Pebl: positive example based learning for web page classification using svm. In *KDD '02: Proceedings of the eighth ACM SIGKDD international conference on Knowledge discovery and data mining*, pages 239–248, New York, NY, USA. ACM.

Anchor Text Extraction for Academic Search

Shuming Shi[1] **Fei Xing**[2*] **Mingjie Zhu**[3*] **Zaiqing Nie**[1] **Ji-Rong Wen**[1]
[1]Microsoft Research Asia
[2]Alibaba Group, China
[3]University of Science and Technology of China
{shumings, znie, jrwen}@microsoft.com
fei_c_xing@yahoo.com; mjzhu@ustc.edu

Abstract

Anchor text plays a special important role in improving the performance of general Web search, due to the fact that it is relatively objective description for a Web page by potentially a large number of other Web pages. Academic Search provides indexing and search functionality for academic articles. It may be desirable to utilize anchor text in academic search as well to improve the search results quality. The main challenge here is that no explicit URLs and anchor text is available for academic articles. In this paper we define and automatically assign a *pseudo-URL* for each academic article. And a machine learning approach is adopted to extract *pseudo-anchor* text for academic articles, by exploiting the citation relationship between them. The extracted pseudo-anchor text is then indexed and involved in the relevance score computation of academic articles. Experiments conducted on 0.9 million research papers show that our approach is able to dramatically improve search performance.

1 Introduction

Anchor text is a piece of clickable text that links to a target Web page. In general Web search, anchor text plays an extremely important role in improving the search quality. The main reason for this is that anchor text actually aggregates the opinion (which is more comprehensive, accurate, and objective) of a potentially large number of people for a Web page.

In recent years, academic search (Giles et al., 1998; Lawrence et al., 1999; Nie et al., 2005; Chakrabarti et al., 2006) has become an important supplement to general web search for retrieving research articles. Several academic search systems (including Google Scholar[†], Citeseer[‡], DBLP[§], Libra[**], ArnetMiner[††], etc.) have been deployed. In order to improve the results quality of an academic search system, we may consider exploiting the techniques which are demonstrated to be quite useful and critical in general Web search. In this paper, we study the possibility of extracting anchor text for research papers and using them to improve the search performance of an academic search system.

> ...commonly cited ranking and scoring algorithms are HITS (Kleinberg 1998) and PageRank (Page et al. 1998), which rank hyperlinked documents using the concepts of hubs and authorities. The most well-known keyword scoring methods within the IR community are the tf-idf (Salton and McGill 1983) and pointwise mutual information (Church and Hanks 1989) measures, which put more importance on matching keywords...

Figure 1. An example of one paper citing other papers

The basic search unit in most academic search systems is a research paper. Borrowing the concepts of URL and anchor-text in general Web search, we may need to assign a *pseudo-URL* for one research paper as its identifier and to define the *pseudo-anchor* text for it by the contextual description when this paper is referenced (or mentioned). The pseudo-URL of a research paper could be the combination of its title, authors and publication information. Figure-1 shows an excerpt where one paper cites a couple of other

[*] This work was performed when *Fei Xing* and *Mingjie Zhu* were interns at Microsoft Research Asia.

[†] http://scholar.google.com/
[‡] http://citeseerx.ist.psu.edu/
[§] http://www.informatik.uni-trier.de/~ley/db/
[**] http://libra.msra.cn/
[††] http://www.arnetminer.org/

Proceedings of the 2009 Workshop on Text and Citation Analysis for Scholarly Digital Libraries, ACL-IJCNLP 2009, pages 10–18, Suntec, Singapore, 7 August 2009.

papers. The grayed text can be treated as the pseudo-anchor text of the papers being referenced. Once the pseudo-anchor text of research papers is acquired, it can be indexed and utilized to help ranking, just as in general web search.

However it remains a challenging task to correctly identify and extract these pseudo-URLs and pseudo-anchor texts. First, unlike the situation in general web search where one unique URL is assigned to each web page as a natural identifier, the information of research papers need to be extracted from web pages or PDF files. As a result, in constructing pseudo-URLs for research papers, we may face the problem of extraction errors, typos, and the case of one research paper having different expressions in different places. Second, in general Web search, anchor text is always explicitly specified by HTML tags (<a> and </a>). It is however much harder to perform anchor text extraction for research papers. For example, human knowledge may be required in Figure-1 to accurately identify the description of every cited paper.

To address the above challenges, we propose an approach for extracting and utilizing pseudo-anchor text information in academic search to improve the search results quality. Our approach is composed of three phases. In the first phase, each time a paper is cited in another paper, we construct a *tentative* pseudo-URL for the cited paper and extract a *candidate anchor block* for it. The tentative pseudo-URL and the candidate anchor block are allowed to be inaccurate. In the second phase, we merge the tentative pseudo-URLs that should represent the same paper. All candidate anchor blocks belong to the same paper are grouped accordingly in this phase. In the third phase, the final pseudo-anchor text of each paper is generated from all its candidate blocks, by adopting a SVM-based machine learning methodology. We conduct experiments upon a dataset containing 0.9 million research papers. The experimental results show that lots of useful anchor text can be successfully extracted and accumulated using our approach, and the ultimate search performance is dramatically improved when anchor information is indexed and used for paper ranking.

The remaining part of this paper is organized as follows. In Section 2, we describe in detail our approach for pseudo-anchor text extraction and accumulation. Experimental results are reported in Section 3. We discuss related work in Section 4 and finally conclude the paper in Section 5.

2 Our Approach

2.1 Overview

Before describing our approach in detail, we first recall how anchor text is processed in general Web search. Assume that there have been a collection of documents being crawled and stored on local disk. In the first step, each web page is parsed and the out links (or forward links) within the page are extracted. Each link is comprised of a URL and its corresponding anchor text. In the second step, all links are accumulated according to their destination URLs (i.e. the anchor texts of all links pointed to the same URL are merged). Thus, we can get all anchor text corresponding to each web page. Figure-2 (a) demonstrates this process.

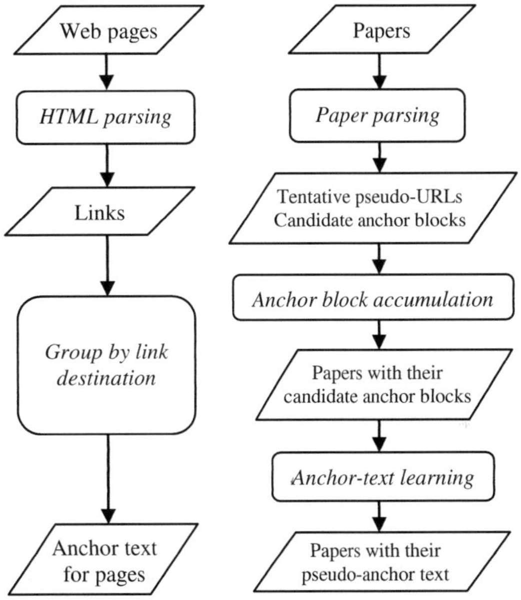

Figure 2. The main process of extracting (a) anchor text in general web search and (b) *pseudo-anchor* text in academic search

For academic search, we need to extract and parse the text content of papers. When a paper *A* mentions another paper *B*, it either explicitly or implicitly displays the key information of *B* to let the users know that it is referencing *B* instead of other papers. Such information can be extracted to construct the *tentative* pseudo-URL of *B*. The pseudo-URLs constructed in this phase are *tentative* because different tentative pseudo-URLs may be merged to generate the same final pseudo-URL. All information related to paper *B* in different papers can be accumulated and treated as the potential anchor text of *B*. Our goal is to get the anchor text related to each paper.

Our approach for pseudo-anchor text extraction is shown in Figure-2 (b). The key process is similar to that in general Web search for accumulating and utilizing page anchor text. One primary difference between Figure-2 (a) and (b) is the latter accumulates candidate anchor blocks rather than pieces of anchor text. A candidate anchor block is a piece of text that contains the description of one paper. The basic idea is: Instead of extracting the anchor text for a paper directly (a difficult task because of the lack of enough information), we first construct a candidate anchor block to contain the "possible" or "potential" description of the paper. After we accumulate all candidate anchor blocks, we have more information to provide a better estimation about which pieces of texts are anchor texts. Following this idea, our proposed approach adopts a three-phase methodology to extract pseudo-anchor text. In the first phase, each time a paper *B* appearing in another paper *A*, a candidate anchor block is extracted for *B*. All candidate anchor blocks belong to the same paper are grouped in the second phase. In the third phase, the final pseudo-anchor text of each paper is selected among all candidate blocks.

Extracting tentative pseudo-URLs and candidate anchor blocks: When one paper cites another paper, a piece of short text (e.g. "[1]" or "(xxx et al., 2008)") is commonly inserted to represent the paper to be cited, and the detail information (key attributes) of it are typically put at the end of the document (in the references section). We call each paper listed in the references section a *reference item*. The references section can be located by searching for the last occurrence of term 'reference' or 'references' in larger fonts. Then, we adopt a rule-based approach to divide the text in the references section into reference items. Another rule-based approach is used to extract paper attributes (title, authors, year, etc) from a reference item. We observed some errors in our resulting pseudo-URLs caused by the quality of HTML files converted from PDF format, reference item extraction errors, paper attribute extraction errors, and other factors. We also observed different reference item formats for the same paper. The pseudo-URL for a paper is defined according to its title, authors, publisher, and publication year, because these four kinds of information can readily be used to identify a paper.

For each citation of a paper, we treat the sentence containing the reference point (or citation point) as one candidate anchor block. When multiple papers are cited in one sentence, we treat the sentence as the candidate anchor block of *every* destination paper.

Candidate Anchor Block Accumulation: This phase is in charge of merging all candidate blocks of the same pseudo-URL. As has been discussed, tentative pseudo-URLs are often inaccurate; and different tentative pseudo-URLs may correspond to the same paper. The primary challenge here is perform the task in an *efficient* way and with high *accuracy*. We will address this problem in Subsection 2.2.

Pseudo-Anchor Generation: In the previous phase, all candidate blocks of each paper have been accumulated. This phase is to generate the final anchor text for each paper from all its candidate blocks. Please refer to Subsection 2.3 for details.

2.2 Candidate Anchor Block Accumulation via Multiple Feature-String Hashing

Consider this problem: Given a potentially huge number of tentative pseudo-URLs for papers, we need to identify and merge the tentative pseudo-URLs that represent the same paper. This is like the problems in the record linkage (Fellegi and Sunter, 1969), entity matching, and data integration which have been extensively studied in database, AI, and other areas. In this sub-section, we will first show the major challenges and the previous similar work on this kind of problem. Then a possible approach is described to achieve a trade-off between accuracy and efficiency.

Pseudo-URL 1:
  Title: E#icient Crawling Through URL Ordering
  Authors: J Cho, H Garcia-Molina, L Page
  PubInfo: WWW7 / Computer Networks
  Year: 1998
Pseudo-URL 2:
  Title: Efficient Crawling Through URL Ordering
  Authors: J Cho, H Garcia-Molina, L Page
  PubInfo: In Proceedings of International World Wide Web Conference

Figure 3. Two tentative pseudo-URLs representing the same paper

2.2.1 *Challenges and candidate techniques*

Two issues should be addressed for this problem: similarity measurement, and the efficiency of the algorithm. On one hand, a proper similarity function is needed to identify two tentative pseudo-URLs representing the same paper. Second, the integration process has to be accomplished efficiently.

We choose to compute the similarity between two papers to be a linear combination of the similarities on the following fields: title, authors, venue (conference/journal name), and year. The similarity function on each field is carefully designed. For paper title, we adopt a term-level edit distance to compute similarity. And for paper authors, person name abbreviation is considered. The similarity function we adopted is fairly well in accuracy (e.g., the similarity between the two pseudo-URLs in Figure-3 is high according to our function); but it is quite time-consuming to compute the similarity for each pair of papers (roughly 10^{12} similarity computation operations are needed for 1 million different tentative pseudo-URLs).

Some existing methods are available for decreasing the times of similarity calculation operations. McCallum et al. (2000) addresses this high dimensional data clustering problem by dividing data into overlapping subsets called canopies according to a cheap, approximate distance measurement. Then the clustering process is performed by measuring the exact distances only between objects from the same canopy. There are also other subspace methods (Parsons et al., 2004) in data clustering areas, where data are divided into subspaces of high dimensional spaces first and then processing is done in these subspaces. Also there are fast blocking approaches for record linkage in Baxter et al. (2003). Though they may have different names, they hold similar ideas of dividing data into subsets to reduce the candidate comparison records. The size of dataset used in the above papers is typically quite small (about thousands of data items). For efficiency issue, Broder et al. (1997) proposed a shingling approach to detect similar Web pages. They noticed that it is infeasible to compare sketches (which are generated by shingling) of all pairs of documents. So they built an inverted index that contains a list of shingle values and the documents they appearing in. With the inverted index, they can effectively generate a list of all the pairs of documents that share any shingles, along with the number of shingles they have in common. They did experiments on a dataset containing 30 million documents.

By adopting the main ideas of the above techniques to our pseudo-URL matching problem, a possible approach can be as follows.

Algorithm Multiple Feature-String Hashing for candidate anchor block accumulation

```
Input: A list of papers (with their tentative pseudo-URLs
and candidate anchor blocks)
Output: Papers with all candidate anchor blocks of the
same paper aggregated

Initial: An empty hashtable h (each slot of h is a list of pa-
pers)
For each paper A in the input list {
  For each feature-string of A {
    Lookup by the feature-string in h to get a slot s;
    Add A into s;
  }
}
For each slot s with size smaller than a threshold {
  For any two papers A1, A2 in s {
    float fSim = Similarity(A1, A2);
    if(fSim > the specified threshold) {
      Merge A1 and A2;
    }
  }
}
```

Figure 4. The Multiple Feature-String Hashing algorithm for candidate anchor block accumulation

2.2.2 *Method adopted*

The method utilized here for candidate anchor block accumulation is shown in Figure 4. The main idea is to construct a certain number of *feature strings* for a tentative pseudo-URL (abbreviated as *TP-URL*) and do hash for the feature strings. A feature string of a paper is a small piece of text which records a part of the paper's key information, satisfying the following conditions: First, multiple feature strings can typically be built from a TP-URL. Second, if two TP-URLs are different representations of the same paper, then the probability that they have at least one common feature string is extremely high. We can choose the term-level *n*-grams of paper titles (referring to Section 3.4) as feature strings.

The algorithm maintains an in-memory hashtable which contains a lot of slots each of which is a list of TP-URLs belonging to this slot. For each TP-URL, feature strings are generated and hashed by a specified hash function. The TP-URL is then added into some slots according to the hash values of its feature strings. Any two TP-URLs belonging to the same slot are further compared by utilizing our similarity function. If their similarity is larger than a threshold, the two TP-URLs are treated as being the same and therefore their corresponding candidate anchor blocks are merged.

The above algorithm tries to achieve good balance between accuracy and performance. On one hand, compared with the naïve algorithm of performing one-one comparison between all pairs of TP-URLs, the algorithm needs only to compute the similarity for the TP-URLs that share a common slot. On the other hand, because of the special property of feature strings, most TP-URLs representing the same paper can be detected and merged.

The basic idea of dividing data into overlapped subsets is inherited from McCallum et al. (2000), Broder et al. (1997), and some subspace clustering approaches. Slightly different, we do not count the number of common feature strings between TP-URLs. Common bins (or inverted indices) between data points are calculated in McCallum et al. (2000) as a "cheap distance" for creating canopies. The number of common Shingles between two Web documents is calculated (efficiently via inverted indices), such that Jaccard similarity could be used to measure the similarity between them. In our case, we simply compare any two TP-URLs in the same slot by using our similarity function directly.

The effective and efficiency of this algorithm depend on the selection of feature strings. For a fixed feature string generation method, the performance of this algorithm is affected by the size of each slot, especially the number and size of big slots (slots with size larger than a threshold). Big slots will be discarded in the algorithm to improve performance, just like removing common Shingles in Broder et al. (1997). In Section 4, we conduct experiments to test the performance of the above algorithm with different feature string functions and different slot size thresholds.

2.3 Pseudo-Anchor Text Learning

In this subsection, we address the problem of extracting the final pseudo-anchor text for a paper, given all its candidate anchor blocks (see Figure 5 for an example).

2.3.1 Problem definition

A candidate anchor block is a piece of text with one or some reference points (a reference point is one occurrence of citation in a paper) specified, where a reference point is denoted by a <*start_pos*, *end_pos*> pair (means start position and end position respectively): *ref* = <*start_pos*, *end_pos*>. We represent a candidate anchor block to be the following format,

$$AnchorBlock = (Text, ref1, ref2, \ldots)$$

We define a *block set* to be a set of candidate anchor blocks for a paper,

$$BlockSet = \{AnchorBlock1, AnchorBlock2, \ldots\}$$

Now the problem is: Given a block set containing N elements, extract some text excerpts from them as the anchor text of the paper.

2.3.2 Learn term weights

We adopt a machine-learning approach to assign, for each *term* in the anchor blocks, a discrete *degree* of being anchor text. The main reasons for taking such an approach is twofold: First, we believe that assigning each term a fuzzy degree of being anchor text is more appropriate than a binary judgment as either an anchor-term or non-anchor-term. Second, since the importance of a term for a "link" may be determined by many factors in paper search, a machine-learning could be more flexible and general than the approaches that compute term degrees by a specially designed formula.

Paper	Scaling personalized web search
Candidate-Anchor text	...Haveliwala **[8]** and Jeh and Widom **[9]** have done work on efficient personalization, observing that the function mapping reset distributions to stationary distributions is linear...
	...A more recent investigation, **[12]**, uses a different approach: it focuses on user profiles...
	...providing personalized ranking of Web pages based on user preferences, while automating the input generation process for the PPR algorithm **[8]**...
	...A partial solution to this scaling problem was given in **[16]**, where the dependence from the number of topics...
	... ...

Figure 5. The candidate pseudo-anchor blocks of a paper

The features used for learning are listed in Table-1.

We observed that it would be more effective if some of the above features are normalized before being used for learning. For a term in candidate anchor block B, its TF are normalized by the BM25 formula (Robertson et al., 1999),

$$TF_{norm} = \frac{(k_1 + 1) \cdot TF}{k_1 \cdot (b + (1-b) \cdot \frac{|B|}{L}) + TF}$$

where L is average length of the candidate blocks, $|B|$ is the length of B, and k_1, b are parameters.

DF is normalized by the following formula,

$$IDF = \log(1 + \frac{N}{DF})$$

where N is the number of elements in the block set (i.e. total number of candidate anchor blocks for the current paper).

Features $RefPos$ and $Dist$ are normalized as,

$$RefPos_{norm} = RefPos \, / \, |B|$$

$$Dist_{norm} = (Dist - RefPos) \, / \, |B|$$

And the feature $BlockLen$ is normalized as,

$BlockLen_{norm} = \log(1{+}BlockLen)$

Features	Description
DF	Document frequency: Number of candidate blocks in which the term appears, counted among all candidate blocks of all papers. It is used to indicate whether the term is a stop word or not.
BF	Block frequency: Number of candidate blocks in which the term appears, counted among all candidate blocks of this paper.
CTF	Collection term frequency: Total number of times the term appearing in the blocks. For multiple times of occurrences in one block, all of them are counted.
IsInURL	Specify whether the term appears in the pseudo-URL of the paper.
TF	Term frequency: Number of times the terms appearing in the candidate block.
Dist	Directed distance from the nearest reference point to the term location
RefPos	Position of the nearest reference point in the candidate pseudo-anchor block.
BlockLen	Length of the candidate pseudo-anchor block

Table 1. Features for learning

We set four term importance levels, from 1 (unrelated terms or stop words) to 4 (words participating in describing the main ideas of the paper).

We choose support vector machine (SVM) for learning term weights here, because of its powerful classification ability and well generalization ability (Burges, 1998). We believe some other machine learning techniques should also work here. The input of the classifier is a feature vector of a term and the output is the importance level of the term. Given a set of training data $\{feature_i, level_i\}_{i=1}^{l}$, a decision function $f(x)$ can be acquired after training. Using the decision function, we can assign an importance level for each term automatically.

3 Experiments

3.1 Experimental Setup

Our experimental dataset contains 0.9 million papers crawled from the web. All the papers are processed according to the process in Figure-2 (b). We randomly select 300 queries from the query log of Libra (libra.msra.cn) and retrieve the results in our indexing and ranking system with/without the pseudo-anchors generated by our approach. Then the volunteer researchers and students in our group are involved to judge the search results. The top 30 results of different ranking algorithms for each query are labeled and assigned a relevance value from 1 (meaning 'poor match') to 5 (meaning 'perfect match'). The search results quality is measured by NDCG (Jarvelin and Kekalainen, 2000).

3.2 Overall Effect of our Approach

Figure 6 shows the performance comparison between the results of two baseline paper ranking algorithms and the results of including pseudo-anchor text in ranking.

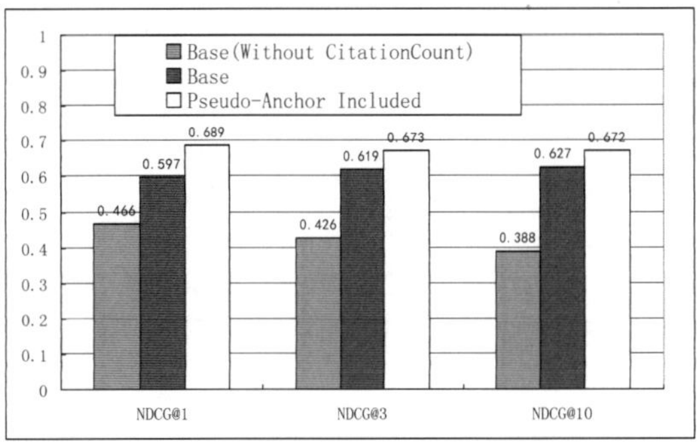

Figure 6. Comparison between the baseline approach and our approach (measure: nDCG)

The "Base" algorithm considers the title, abstract, full-text and static-rank (which is a function of the citation count) of a paper. In a bit more detail, for each paper, we adopt the BM25 formula (Robertson et al., 1999) over its title, abstract, and full-text respectively. And then the resulting score is linearly combined with the static-rank to get its final score. The static-rank is computed as follows,

$$StaticRank = \log(1{+}CitationCount) \tag{3.1}$$

To test the performance of including pseudo-anchor text in ranking, we compute an anchor score for each paper and linearly combine it with its baseline score (i.e. the score computed by the baseline algorithm).

We tried two kinds of ways for anchor score computation. The first is to merge all pieces of anchor excerpts (extracted in the previous section) into a larger piece of anchor text, and use BM25 to compute its relevance score. In another approach called homogeneous evidence combination (Shi et al., 2006), a relevance score is computed for each anchor excerpt (still using BM25), and all the scores for the excerpts are sorted descending and then combined by the following formula,

$$S_{anchor} = \sum_{i=1}^{m} \frac{1}{(1+c\cdot(i-1))^2} \cdot s_i \tag{3.2}$$

where s_i (i=1, …, m) are scores for the m anchor excerpts, and c is a parameter. The primary idea here is to let larger scores to have relative greater weights. Please refer to Shi et al. (2006) for a justification of this approach. As we get slightly better results with the latter way, we use it as our final choice for computing anchor scores.

From Figure 6, we can see that the overall performance is greatly improved by including pseudo-anchor information. Table 2 shows the t-test results, where a ">" indicates that the algorithm in the row outperforms that in the column with a *p*-value of 0.05 or less, and a ">>" means a *p*-value of 0.01 or less.

	Base	**Base (without CitationCount)**
Our approach	>	>>
Base		>>
Base (without CitationCount)		

Table 2. Statistical significance tests (t-test over nDCG@3)

Table 3 shows the performance comparison by using some traditional IR measures based on binary judgments. Since the results of not including CitationCount are much worse than the other two, we omit it in the table.

Approach \ Measure	**MAP**	**MRR**	**P@1**	**P@10**
Base (including CitationCount)	0.364	0.727	0.613	0.501
Our Approach	0.381	0.734	0.625	0.531

Table 3. Performance compassion using binary judgment measures

3.3 Sample Query Analysis

Here we analyze some sample queries to get some insights about why and how pseudo-anchor improves search performance. Figure-7 and Figure-8 show the top-3 results of two sample queries: {TF-IDF} and {Page Rank}.

For query "TF-IDF", the top results of the baseline approach have keyword "TF-IDF" appeared in the title as well as in other places of the papers. Although the returned papers are relevant to the query, they are not excellent because typically users may want to get the first TF-IDF paper or some papers introducing TF-IDF. When pseudo-anchor information is involved, some excellent results (B1, B2, B3) are generated. The main reason for getting the improved results is that these papers (or books) are described with "TF-IDF" when lots of other papers cite them.

A1. K Sugiyama, K Hatano, M Yoshikawa, S Uemura. **Refinement of TF-IDF schemes for web pages using their hyperlinked neighboring pages**. Hypertext'03
A2. A Aizawa. **An information-theoretic perspective of tf-idf measures**. IPM'03.
A3. N Oren. **Reexamining tf.idf based information retrieval with Genetic Programming**. SAICSIT'02.

(a) Without anchor

B1. G Salton, MJ McGill. **Introduction to Modern Information Retrieval**. McGraw-Hill, 1983.
B2. G Salton and C Buckley. **Term weighting approaches in automatic text retrieval**. IPM'98.
B3. R Baeza-Yates, B Ribeiro-Neto. **Modern Information Retrieval**. Addison-Wesley, 1999

(b) With anchor

Figure 7. Top-3 results for query TF-IDF

A1. V Safronov, M Parashar, Y Wang et al. **Optimizing Web servers using Page rank prefetching for clustered accesses**. Information Sciences. 2003.
A2. AO Mendelzon, D Rafiei. **An autonomous page ranking method for metasearch engines**. WWW, 2002.
A3. FB Kalhoff. **On formally real Division Algebras and Quasifields of Rank two**.

(a) Without anchor

B1. S Brin, L Page. **The Anatomy of a Large-Scale Hypertextual Web Search Engine**. WWW, 1998
B2. L Page, S Brin, R Motwani, T Winograd. **The pagerank citation ranking: Bringing order to the web**. 1998.
B3. JM Kleinberg. **Authoritative sources in a hyperlinked environment**. Journal of the ACM, 1999.

(b) With anchor

Figure 8. Top-3 results for query Page Rank

Figure-8 shows another example about how pseudo-anchor helps to improve search results quality. For query "Page Rank" (note that there is a space in between), the results returned by the baseline approach are not satisfactory. In the papers returned by our approach, at least B1 and B2 are very good results. Although they did not label themselves "Page Rank", other papers do so in citing them. Interestingly, although the result B3 is not about the "PageRank" algorithm, it describes another popular "Page Rank" algorithm in addition to PageRank.

Another interesting observation from the two figures is that our approach retrieves older papers than the baseline method, because old papers tend to have more anchor text (due to more citations). So our approach may not be suitable for retrieve newer papers. To overcome this problem, maybe publication year should be considered in our ranking functions.

3.4 Anchor Accumulation Experiments

We conduct experiments to test the effectiveness and efficiency of the multiple-feature-string-hashing algorithm presented in Section 2.2. The duplication detection quality of this algorithm is determined by the appropriate selection of feature strings. When feature strings are fixed, the slot size threshold can be used to tune the tradeoff between accuracy and performance.

Feature Strings / Slot Distr.	Ungram	Bigram	Trigram	4-gram
# of Slots	$1.4*10^5$	$1.2*10^6$	$2.8*10^6$	$3.4*10^6$
# of Slots with size > 100	5240	6806	1541	253
# of Slots with size > 1000	998	363	50	5
# of Slots with size > 10000	59	11	0	0

Table 4. Slot distribution with different feature strings

We take all the papers extracted from PDF files as input to run the algorithm. Identical TP-URLs are first eliminated (therefore their candidate anchor blocks are merged) by utilizing a hash table. This pre-process step results in about 1.46 million distinct TP-URLs. The number is larger than our collection size (0.9 million), because some cited papers are not in our paper collection. We tested four kinds of feature strings all of which are generated from paper title: unigrams, bigrams, trigrams, and 4-grams. Table-4 shows the slot size distribution corresponding to each kind of feature strings. The performance comparison among different feature strings and slot size thresholds is shown in Table 5. It seems that bigrams achieve a good trade-off between accuracy and performance.

Feature Strings	Slot Size Threshold	Dup. papers Detected	Processing Time (sec)
Unigram	5000	529,717	119,739.0
	500	327,357	7,552.7
Bigram	500	528,981	8,229.6
Trigram	Infinite	518,564	8,420.4
	500	516,369	2,654.9
4-gram	500	482,299	1,138.2

Table 5. Performance comparison between different feature strings and slot size thresholds

4 Related Work

There has been some work which uses anchor text or their surrounding text for various Web information retrieval tasks. It was known at the very beginning era of internet that anchor text was useful to Web search (McBryan, 1994). Most Web search engines now use anchor text as primary and power evidence for improving search performance. The idea of using contextual text in a certain vicinity of the anchor text was proposed in Chakrabarti et al. (1998) to automatically compile some lists of authoritative Web resources on a range of topics. An anchor window approach is proposed in Chakrabarti et al (1998) to extract implicit anchor text. Following this work, anchor windows were considered in some other tasks (Amitay et al., 1998; Haveliwala et al., 2002; Davison, 2002; Attardi et al., 1999). Although we are inspired by these ideas, our work is different because research papers have many different properties from Web pages. From the viewpoint of implicit anchor extraction techniques, our approach is different from the anchor window approach. The anchor window approach is somewhat simpler and easy to implement than ours. However, our method is more general and flexible. In our approach, the anchor text is not necessarily to be in a window.

Citeseer (Giles et al., 1998; Lawrence et al., 1999) has been doing a lot of valuable work on citation recognition, reference matching, and paper indexing. It has been displaying contextual information for cited papers. This feature has been shown to be helpful and useful for researchers. Differently, we are using context description for improving ranking rather than display purpose. In addition to Citeseer, some other work (McCallum et al., 1999; Nanba and Okumura, 1999; Nanba et al., 2004; Shi et al., 2006) is also available for extracting and accumulating reference information for research papers.

5 Conclusions and Future Work

In this paper, we propose to improve academic search by utilizing pseudo-anchor information. As pseudo-URL and pseudo-anchor text are not as explicit as in general web search, more efforts are needed for pseudo-anchor extraction. Our machine-learning approach has proven successful in automatically extracting implicit anchor text. By using the pseudo-anchors in our academic search system, we see a significant performance improvement over the basic approach.

Acknowledgments
We would like to thank Yunxiao Ma and Pu Wang for converting paper full-text from PDF to HTML format. Jian Shen has been helping us do some reference extraction and matching work. Special thanks are given to the researchers and students taking part in data labeling.

References

E. Amitay. 1998. Using common hypertext links to identify the best phrasal description of target web documents. In Proc. of the SIGIR'98 Post Conference Workshop on Hypertext Information Retrieval for the Web, Melbourne, Australia.

G. Attardi, A. Gulli, and F. Sebastiani. 1999. Theseus: categorization by context. In Proceedings of the 8th International World Wide Web Conference.

A. Baxter, P. Christen, T. Churches. 2003. A comparison of fast blocking methods for record linkage. In ACM SIGKDD'03 Workshop on Data Cleaning, Record Linkage and Object consolidation. Washington DC.

A. Broder, S. Glassman, M. Manasse, and G. Zweig. 1997. Syntactic clustering of the Web. In Proceedings of the Sixth International World Wide Web Conference, pp. 391-404.

C.J.C. Burges. 1998. A tutorial on support vector machines for pattern recognition. Data Mining and Knowledge Discovery, 2, 121-167.

S. Chakrabarti, B. Dom, D. Gibson, J. Kleinberg, P. Raghavan, and S. Rajagopalan. 1998. Automatic resource list compilation by analyzing hyperlink structure and associated text. In Proceedings of the 7th International World Wide Web Conference.

K. Chakrabarti, V. Ganti, J. Han, and D. Xin. 2006. Ranking objects based on relationships. In SIGMOD '06: Proceedings of the 2006 ACM SIGMOD international conference on Management of data, pages 371–382, New York, NY, USA. ACM.

B. Davison. 2000. Topical locality in the web. In SIGIR'00: Proceedings of the 23rd annual international ACM SIGIR conference on Research and development in information retrieval, pages 272-279, New York, NY, USA. ACM.

I.P. Fellegi, and A.B. Sunter. A Theory for Record Linkage, Journal of the American Statistical Association, 64, (1969), 1183-1210.

C. L. Giles, K. Bollacker, and S. Lawrence. 1998. CiteSeer: An automatic citation indexing system. In IanWitten, Rob Akscyn, and Frank M. Shipman III, editors, Digital Libraries 98 - The Third ACM Conference on Digital Libraries, pages 89–98, Pittsburgh, PA, June 23–26. ACM Press.

T.H. Haveliwala, A. Gionis, D. Klein, and P. Indyk. 2002. Evaluating strategies for similarity search on the web. In WWW '02: Proceedings of the 11th international conference on World Wide Web, pages 432–442, New York, NY, USA. ACM.

K. Jarvelin, and J. Kekalainen. 2000. IR Evaluation Methods for Retrieving Highly Relevant Documents. In Proceedings of the 23rd Annual International ACM SIGIR Conference on Research and Development in Information Retrieval (SIGIR2000).

S. Lawrence, C.L. Giles, and K. Bollacker. 1999. Digital libraries and Autonomous Citation Indexing. IEEE Computer, 32(6):67–71.

A. McCallum, K. Nigam, J. Rennie, and K. Seymore. 1999. Building Domain-specific Search Engines with Machine Learning Techniques. In Proceedings of the AAAI-99 Spring Symposium on Intelligent Agents in Cyberspace.

A. McCallum, K. Nigam, and L. Ungar. 2000. Efficient clustering of high-dimensional data sets with application to reference matching. In Proc. 6th ACM SIGKDD Int. Conf. on Knowledge Discovery and Data Mining.

O.A. McBryan. 1994. Genvl and wwww: Tools for taming the web. In In Proceedings of the First International World Wide Web Conference, pages 79-90.

H. Nanba, M. Okumura. 1999. Towards Multi-paper Summarization Using Reference Information. In Proc. of the 16th International Joint Conference on Artificial Intelligence, pp.926-931.

H. Nanba, T. Abekawa, M. Okumura, and S. Saito. 2004. Bilingual PRESRI: Integration of Multiple Research Paper Databases. In Proc. of RIAO 2004, 195-211.

L. Parsons, E. Haque, H. Liu. 2004. Subspace clustering for high dimensional data: a review. SIGKDD Explorations 6(1): 90-105.

S.E. Robertson, S. Walker, and M. Beaulieu. 1999. Okapi at TREC-7: automatic ad hoc, filtering, VLC and filtering tracks. In Proceedings of TREC'99.

S. Shi, R. Song, and J-R Wen. 2006. Latent Additivity: Combining Homogeneous Evidence. Technique report, MSR-TR-2006-110, Microsoft Research, August 2006.

S. Shi, F. Xing, M. Zhu, Z.Nie, and J.-R. Wen. 2006. Pseudo-Anchor Extraction for Search Vertical Objects. In Proc. of the 2006 ACM 15th Conference on Information and Knowledge Management. Arlington, USA.

Z. Nie, Y. Zhang, J.-R. Wen, and W.-Y. Ma. 2005. Object-level ranking: bringing order to web objects. InWWW'05: Proceedings of the 14th international conference on World Wide Web, pages 567–574, New York, NY, USA. ACM.

Accurate Argumentative Zoning with Maximum Entropy models

Stephen Merity and **Tara Murphy** and **James R. Curran**
School of Information Technologies
University of Sydney
NSW 2006, Australia
{smerity,tm,james}@it.usyd.edu.au

Abstract

We present a maximum entropy classifier that significantly improves the accuracy of *Argumentative Zoning* in scientific literature. We examine the features used to achieve this result and experiment with Argumentative Zoning as a sequence tagging task, decoded with Viterbi using up to four previous classification decisions. The result is a 23% F-score increase on the Computational Linguistics conference papers marked up by Teufel (1999).

Finally, we demonstrate the performance of our system in different scientific domains by applying it to a corpus of Astronomy journal articles annotated using a modified Argumentative Zoning scheme.

1 Introduction

The task of generating automatic summarizations of one or more texts is a central problem in Natural Language Processing (NLP). Summarization is a fundamental component for future information retrieval and question answering systems, incorporating both natural language understanding and natural language generation.

Comprehension-based summarization, e.g. Kintsch and Van Dijk (1978) and Brown et al. (1983), is the most ambitious model of automatic summarization, requiring a complete understanding of the text. Due to the failure of rule-based NLP and knowledge representation, other less knowledge-intensive methods now dominate.

Sentence extraction, e.g. Brandow et al. (1995) and Kupiec et al. (1995), selects a small number of abstract worthy sentences from a larger text. The resulting sentences form a collection of excerpt sentences meant to capture the essence of the text. The next stage is information fusion (Barzilay et al., 1999; Knight and Marcu, 2000) which attempts to combine the excerpts into a more cohesive text. These methods can create inflexible and incoherent extracts that result in under-informative results (Teufel et al., 1999).

Argumentative Zoning (Teufel, 1999; Teufel and Moens, 2002) attempts to solve this problem by representing the structure of a text using a rhetorically-based schema. Sentences are classified into one of a small number of non-hierarchical argumentative roles, which can then be used in both the sentence extraction and text generation/fusion phase of automatic summarization. Argumentative Zoning can enable tailored summarizations depending on the needs of the user, e.g. a layperson versus a domain expert.

The first experiments in Argumentative Zoning used Naïve Bayes (NB) classifiers (Kupiec et al., 1995; Teufel, 1999) which assume conditional independence of the features. However, this assumption is rarely true for the kinds of rich feature representations we want to use for most NLP tasks.

Maximum entropy (ME) models have become popular in NLP because they can incorporate evidence from the complex, diverse and overlapping features needed to represent language. Some example applications include part-of-speech (POS) tagging (Ratnaparkhi, 1996), parsing (Johnson et al., 1999), language modelling (Rosenfeld, 1996), and text categorisation (Nigam et al., 1999).

We have developed an Argumentative Zoning (*zone*) classifier using a ME model. We compare our zone classifier to a reimplementation of Teufel and Moens (2002)'s NB classifier and features on their original Computational Linguistics corpus. Like Teufel (1999), we model zone classification as a sequence tagging task. Our zone classifier achieves an F-score of 96.88%, a 20% improvement. We also show how Argumentative Zoning can be applied to other domains by evaluating our system on a corpus of Astronomy journal articles, achieving an F-measure of 97.9%.

Proceedings of the 2009 Workshop on Text and Citation Analysis for Scholarly Digital Libraries, ACL-IJCNLP 2009, pages 19–26,
Suntec, Singapore, 7 August 2009.

Category	Abbr.	Description
Background	**BKG**	general scientific background
Other	**OTH**	neutral descriptions of other researcher's work
Own	**OWN**	neutral descriptions of the authors' new work
Aim	**AIM**	statements of the particular aim of the current paper
Textual	**TXT**	statements of textual organisation of the current paper
Contrast	**CTR**	contrastive or comparative statements about other work explicit mention of weaknesses of other work
Basis	**BAS**	statements that own work is based on other work

Table 1: Teufel's (1999) Argumentative Zones

2 Argumentative Zoning

Teufel (1999) introduced a new rhetorical analysis for scientific texts called *Argumentative Zoning*. Each sentence of an article from the scientific literature is classified into one of seven basic rhetorical structures shown in Table 1.

The first three: Background, Other, and Own, are part of the basic schema and represent attribution of intellectual ownership. The four additional categories: aim, textual, contrast, and basis, are based upon Swales (1990)'s Creating A Research Space (CARS) model, and provide pointed information about the author's stance and the paper itself. Teufel assumes that each sentence only requires a single classification and that all sentences clearly fit into the above structure. The assumption is clearly not always correct, but is a useful approximation nevertheless.

Due to the specific nature of these classifications it is hoped that this will allow for much more robust automatic abstraction generation. Summaries of a paper could be created specifically for the user, either focusing on the aim of the work, the work's stance in the field (what other works it is based upon or compared with) and so on.

Teufel used Argumentative Zoning to determine the author's use and opinion of other authors they cite in their work and also to create *Rhetorical Document Profiles* (RDP), a type of summarization used to provide typical information that a new reader may need in a systematic manner.

For the use of Argumentative Zoning in RDPs Teufel (1999) points out that due to the redundancy in language that near perfect accuracy is not required as important pieces of information will be repeated in the paper. Recognising these salient points once is enough for them to be included in the RDP. In further tasks, such as the analysis of the function of citations (Teufel et al., 2006) and automatic summarization, higher levels of accuracy are more critical.

3 Maximum Entropy models

Maximum entropy (ME) or log-linear models are statistical models that can incorporate evidence from a diverse range of complex and potentially overlapping features. Unlike Naïve Bayes (NB), the features can be conditionally dependent given the class, which is important since feature sets in NLP rarely satisfy this independence constraint.

The ME classifier uses models of the form:

$$p(y|x) = \frac{1}{Z(x)} \exp\left(\sum_{i=1}^{n} \lambda_i f_i(x, y)\right) \quad (1)$$

where y is the zone label, x is the context (the sentence) and the $f_i(x, y)$ are the *features* with associated weights λ_i.

The probability of a sequence of zone labels $y_1 \ldots y_n$ given a sequence of sentences is $s_1 \ldots s_n$ is approximated as follows:

$$p(y_1 \ldots y_n | s_1 \ldots s_n) \approx \prod_{i=1}^{n} p(y_i|x_i) \quad (2)$$

where x_i is the context for sentence s_i. In our experiments that treat argumentative zoning as a sequence labelling task, the context x_i incorporates history information – i.e. the previous labelling decisions of the classifier. Optimal decoding of this sequence uses the Viterbi algorithm, which we compare against the Oracle case of knowing the correct label for the previous sentence.

The features are binary valued functions which pair a zone label with various elements of the sentential context; for example:

$$f_j(x, y) = \begin{cases} 1 & \text{if } \texttt{goal} \in x \ \& \ y = \texttt{AIM} \\ 0 & \text{otherwise} \end{cases} \quad (3)$$

$\texttt{goal} \in x$, that is, the word `goal` is part of the context of the sentence, is a *contextual predicate*.

The central idea in maximum entropy modelling is that the model chosen should satisfy all of the constraints imposed by the training data (in the form of empirical feature counts from the training data) whilst remaining as unbiased as possible. This is achieved by selecting the model with the maximum entropy, i.e. the most uniform distribution, given the constraints.

Our classifier uses the maximum entropy implementation described in Curran and Clark (2003). Generalised Iterative Scaling (GIS) is used to estimate the values of the weights and we use a Gaussian prior over the weights (Chen and Rosenfeld, 1999) which allows many rare, but informative, features to be used without overfitting. This will be an important property when we use sparse features like bigrams in the models below.

4 Modelling Argumentative Zones

4.1 Our Features

The two primary sources of features for our zone classifier were the words in the sentences and the position of the sentence relative to the rest of the paper. A number of feature types use additional external resources (e.g. semantic lists of agents or common rhetorical patterns) or annotations (e.g. named entities). Where feasible we have reimplemented the features described in Teufel (1999). In other cases, our features are somewhat simpler.

Since the Curran and Clark (2003) classifier only accepts binary features, any numerical features had to be bucketed into smaller sets of alternatives to reduce sparseness, either by integer division or through reducing the number by scaling to a small integer range. The features we implemented are described below.

Unigrams, bigrams and n-grams

A sub-sequence of *n* words from a given sentence. We include unigram and bigram features and report them individually and together (as n-grams). These features include all of the unigrams and bigrams above the feature cutoff, unlike Teufel's cont-1 features below. Also, both the Computational Linguistics and Astronomy corpora contain marked up citations, cross-references to tables, figures, and sections and mathematical expressions. In the Computational Linguistics corpus self citations are distinguished from other citations. These structured elements have been normalised to a single token each, e.g. `__CITE__`. These tokens have been retained in the unigram and bigram features.

first The first four words of a sentence, added individually.

Sections, positions, and lengths

section A section counter which increments on each heading to measure the distance into the document. It does not take into consideration whether they are sub-headings or similar. There are two versions of this feature. The first is a straight counter (1 to n) and the second is grouped into two buckets representing each half of the paper (breaking at the middle section).

location The position of a sentence between two headings (representing a section). There are two versions of this feature, one counts to a maximum of 10 and the other represents a percentage through the section bucketed into 20% intervals.

paragraph The position of the sentence within a paragraph. Again there are two features – either straight counts (with a maximum of 10) or bucketed into thirds of a paragraph.

length of sentence grouped into multiples of 3.

Named entity features

Our astronomy corpus has been manually annotated with domain-specific named entity information (Murphy et al., 2006). There are 12 coarse-grained categories and 43 fine-grained categories including star, galaxy, telescope, as well as a number of the usual categories including person, organisation and location. Both the coarse-grained and fine-grained categories were used as features.

4.2 Teufel (1999)'s features

To compare with previous work, we also implemented most of the features that gave Teufel (1999) the best performance. We list all of the feature types in Table 2, indicating which ones have and have not been implemented.

Teufel's unigram features (**cont-1**) are filtered using TF-IDF to select the top scoring 10 words in each document, and then these are used to mark the top 40 sentences in each document containing those filtered words.

TLoc marks the position of the sentence over the entire paper, using 10 unevenly sized segments (larger segments are in the middle of the paper).

Struct-1 marks where a sentence appears in a section. It divides each section into three equally sized segments; singles out the first and the last sentence as separate segments; the second and

Name	Impl?	Description
Cont-1	yes	An application of TF-IDF over the words and sentences
Cont-2	partial	Does the sentence contain words in the title or heading (excluding stop words)
TLoc	yes	Position of the sentence in relation to 10 segments (A-J)
Struct-1	yes	Position within a section
Struct-2	yes	Relative position of sentence within a paragraph
Struct-3	partial	Type of headline of the current section
TLength	yes	Is the sentence longer than 15 words?
Syn-1	no	Voice of the first finite verb in the sentence
Syn-2	no	Tense of the first finite verb in the sentence
Syn-3	no	Is the first finite verb modified by a modal auxiliary
Cit-1	yes	Does the sentence contain a citation or name of author?
Formu	yes	Does a formulaic expression occur in the sentence
Ag-1	yes	Type of agent
Ag-2	yes	Type of action (with or without negation)

Table 2: Teufel (1999)'s set of features

third sentence as a sixth segment; and the second-last plus third-last sentence as a seventh segment. **Struct-3** the type of section heading for the current section. In our case, we have not mapped these down to the reduced set used by Teufel.

Formu uses pattern matching rules to identify formulaic expressions. **Ag-1** and **Ag-2** identify agent and action expressions from gazetteers. Teufel (1999) provides these in the appendices.

4.3 Feature Cutoff

Features that occur rarely in the training set are problematic because the statistics extracted for these features are not reliable. They may still contribute positively to the ME model because we use Gaussian smoothing (Chen and Rosenfeld, 1999) help avoid overfitting.

Instead of including every possible feature, we used a cutoff to remove features that occur less than four times. This primarily applies to the n-gram features, especially bigrams, which were quite sparse given the small quantity of training data. Due to the speed of the ME implementation it is possible to have quite a low cut-off.

4.4 History features and Viterbi

In order to take advantage of the predictability of tags given prior sequences (for example, AIM commonly following itself) we used history features and treated Argumentative Zoning as a sequence labelling task. Since each prediction now relies on the previous decisions we used the Viterbi algorithm to find the optimal sequence.

Given the small number of labelling alternatives, we experimented with several history lengths ranging from previous label to the previous four labels. To determine the impact of this feature in an ideal situation, we also experimented with using an Oracle set of history features.

5 Results

Our results are produced using ten-fold cross validation and are reported in terms of precision, recall and f-score for each of the zone classes, and a weighted average over all classes. We have investigated the impact of each feature type using subtractive analysis, where we have also calculated paired t-test confidence intervals (the error values reported are the 95% confidence interval).

The baselines for both sets were already quite high (at least 70%) due to the common tag of OWN, representing the author's own work, but our results show significant improvements over this baseline.

5.1 CMP-LG Corpus

The CMP-LG corpus is a collection of 80 conference papers collected by Teufel (1999) from the Computation and Language E-Print Archive [1]. The LaTeX source was converted to HTML with Latex2HTML then transformed into XML with custom PERL scripts. This text was then tokenized using the TTT (Text Tokenization) System into Penn Treebank format. The result is a corpus of 12,000 annotated sentences, containing 333,000 word tokens, in XML format.

We attempted to recreate Teufel's original experiments by emulating the features she used with the same type of classifier. We used Weka's (Frank et al., 2005) implementation of the NB classifier.

Table 3 reproduces the results from Teufel and Moens (2002) alongside our reimplementation of

[1] `http://xxx.lanl.gov/cmp-lg/`

Tag	original P	R	F	reproduced P	R	F
AIM	44	65	52	45.8	57.8	51.1
BAS	37	40	38	23.8	37.0	28.9
CTR	34	20	26	33.1	19.2	24.3
BKG	40	50	45	46.9	53.6	50.1
OTH	52	39	44	70.6	55.0	61.8
TXT	57	66	61	66.3	47.6	55.4
OWN	84	88	86	86.7	90.8	88.7
Weighted	72	73	72	76.8	76.8	76.8

Table 3: Teufel and Moens (2002)'s and our NB performance on CMP-LG

History Type	Order	Performance	
Baseline	None	93.16	
Viterbi	First	1.77	± 0.49%
Viterbi	Second	1.97	± 0.42%
Viterbi	Third	2.08	± 0.45%
Viterbi	Fourth	2.1	± 0.46%
Viterbi	Fifth	2.13	± 0.46%
Oracle	First	3.67	± 0.68%
Oracle	Second	4.06	± 0.70%

Table 4: History features on the CMP-LG corpus with ME model of unigram/bigram features only

Feature	Classifier	Viterbi
Ngrams	-21.39±2.35%	-23.23±3.24%
Unigram	-8.00±1.02%	-7.53±1.14%
Bigram	-7.89±1.20%	-6.87±1.44%
Concept	-0.06±0.24%	-0.06±0.16%
First	-1.24±0.44%	-1.14±0.39%
Length	-0.34±0.24%	-0.40±0.25%
Section	-0.42±0.27%	-0.27±0.33%
Location	0.03±0.20%	0.04±0.07%
Paragraph	0.10±0.15%	0.01±0.08%
All	95.69%	96.88%

Table 5: Subtractive analysis CMP-LG ME model

the features using Weka's NB classifier. We have been able to replicate their results to a reasonable extent – gaining higher overall performance using most of their original features. Notably, our Other class is significantly more accurate whilst the original Basis class did better.

Our next experiment investigated the value of treating Argumentative Zoning as a sequence labelling task, i.e. the impact of the Markov history features and Viterbi decoding on performance. For these experiments we only used the unigram and bigram features with the maximum entropy classifier. Table 4 presents the results: the baseline is already much higher than the NB classifier which is a result of both the unigram/bigram features and the ME classifier itself.

The improvement using longer Markov windows (up to 2.13%) is also shown – and longer windows are better, although there is diminishing returns. We chose a Markov history of the four previous decisions for the rest of our experiments. Table 4 also shows that knowing the previous label perfectly (with the Oracle experiment) can make a large difference to classification accuracy.

Feature	Change
TLength	-2.09±9.96%
Struct-1	0.38±6.08%
TLoc	0.96±7.25%
Struct-3	-1.65±6.76%
Cont-2	-1.10±6.39%
Struct-2	1.59±7.99%
Ag-1/2	-0.39±8.97%
Formu	0.14±8.46%
Cit-1	-1.88±5.19%
Cont-1	-0.38±5.85%
All	70.25%

Table 6: Teufel's Subtractive analysis CMP-LG ME

Table 5 presents the subtractive analysis to determine the impact of different feature types. From this we can see that the n-grams (unigrams and bigrams) have by far the largest impact – and neither of these feature types was directly implemented by Teufel and Moens (2002). The next most important features are the first few words (again a unigram type feature), length and the section number. The Markov history features also have an impact of just over 1%.

Table 6 shows a different story for Teufel's features using the maximum entropy model. It seems that none of the feature types alone are making an enormous contribution and that the impact of them varies enormously between folds (the confidence intervals are far bigger than the differences).

Finally, Table 7 gives the results of using the maximum entropy model with Markov history length four and all of the features. Overall, we improve Teufel and Moens' performance by just under 20% on our reproduced experiments.

5.2 Astronomical Corpus

The astronomical corpus was created by Murphy et al. (2006) and consists of papers obtained from arXiv (2005)'s astrophysics section (astro-ph). The papers were converted from LaTeX to Unicode by a custom script which attempted to retain as much of the paper's special characters and formatting as possible.

The resulting text was then processed using MXTerminator (Reynar and Ratnaparkhi, 1997) with an additional Python script to find sentence

Category	Abbr.	Description
Background	**BKG**	As has been noted in prior studies , Abell|GXYC 2255|GXYC has an unusually large number of galaxies with extended radio emission .
Other	**OTH**	This is consistent with the findings of Hogg|P Fruchter|P (1999|DAT) who found that GRB hosts are in general subluminous galaxies .
Own	**OWN**	We scanned the data of about 1.8|DUR year|DUR (TJDs|DUR 11000-11699|DUR) and found 30 new GRB-like events .
Data	**DAT**	In Fig . __REF__ we present the 1.4|FRQ GHz|FRQ radio images of the cluster A2744|GXYC , at different angular resolutions . *(subclassed from OWN)*
Observation	**OBS**	Smith|P et al. (2001|DAT) reported no detection of transient emission at sub-mm (850|WAV um|WAV) wavelengths . *(subclassed from OTH)*
Technique	**TEC**	Reduction of the NIR images was performed with the IRAF|CODE and STSDAS|CODE packages . *(subclassed from OWN)*

Figure 1: Examples of sentences with the given tags in the astronomical corpus

Tag	P	R	F
AIM	96.5	88.2	92.2
BAS	86.7	89.8	88.2
CTR	92.1	89.0	90.5
BKG	86.0	96.3	90.9
OTH	96.3	91.7	93.9
TXT	98.2	93.8	95.9
OWN	98.6	99.2	98.9
Weighted	96.88	96.88	96.88

Table 7: Final CMP-LG ME performance

Feature	Classifier	Viterbi
Ngrams	-18.83±3.74%	-16.03±2.99%
Unigram	-5.51±1.37%	-5.25±2.00%
Bigram	-2.04±0.78%	-1.79±0.87%
Concept	-0.18±0.29%	-0.05±0.12%
Entity	-0.18±0.39%	-0.31±0.23%
First	-0.02±0.29%	-0.86±0.79%
Length	-0.06±0.16%	-0.08±0.10%
Paragraph	-0.04±0.20%	0.07±0.19%
Section	-0.29±0.24%	-0.40±0.57%
Location	-0.09±0.25%	0.06±0.15%
All	98.15%	96.68%

Table 8: Subtractive analysis ASTRO ME model

boundaries, and then tokenized using the Penn Treebank (Marcus et al., 1993) sed script, with another Python script fixing common errors. The LaTeX, which the tokenizer split off incorrectly, was then reattached.

Each sentence of the corpus was then annotated using a modified version of the Argumentative Zoning schema. While the original three zones: Background, Own, Other are used, we have replaced the CARS labels with content labels describing aspects of the work: **DAT** for data used in the analysis, **OBS** for observations performed, and **TEC** for techniques applied. Only Own and Other are subclassed with the extended schema of Data, Observation and Techniques. Examples of each zone classification are shown in Figure 1.

Tag	P	R	F
BKG	92.1	97.1	94.5
OTH	95.0	97.1	96.1
OTH-DAT	100.0	92.3	96.0
OTH-OBS	91.3	93.3	92.3
OTH-TEC	100.0	100.0	100.0
OWN	99.9	99.3	99.6
OWN-DAT	95.9	86.6	91.0
OWN-OBS	98.2	89.4	93.6
OWN-TEC	90.4	100.0	94.9
Weighted	97.9	97.9	97.9

Table 9: Final ASTRO ME model performance

Table 8 shows the impact of different feature types on classification accuracy for the Astronomy corpus. Again, the most important features are the n-grams (although to a slightly lesser extent than for the Computational Linguistics corpus). The other features make very little contribution at all. Disappointingly, the (gold-standard) named entity features contribute very little additional information – which is surprising given that the content categories (data and observation) are directly connected with some of the entity types (like telescope).

In the Astronomy corpus, the Markov history features actually have a detrimental effect, which suggests the history is misleading. This warrants further exploration, but we suspect there may be more changing backwards and forwards between argumentative zones in the Astronomy corpus. Overall, we can see that the two tasks are of a similar level of difficulty of around 96% F-score.

Table 9 shows the distribution over zones and content labels for the Astronomy corpus. The Background label is the hardest to reproduce even though it is not split into content sub-types. The sub-types are relatively rare for Other, so the results should not be considered as reliable.

Tag	P	R	F
BKG NB CMP-LG	51.5%	61.1%	55.9%
OTH NB CMP-LG	73.0%	64.2%	68.3%
OWN NB CMP-LG	91.9%	93.1%	92.5%
BKG NB ASTRO	63.1%	63.5%	63.3%
OTH NB ASTRO	53.9%	39.7%	45.7%
OWN NB ASTRO	88.5%	93.0%	90.7%
BKG ME CMP-LG	53.6%	27.5%	36.3%
OTH ME CMP-LG	63.0%	24.4%	35.2%
OWN ME CMP-LG	81.7%	96.8%	88.6%
BKG ME ASTRO	61.2%	29.5%	39.8%
OTH ME ASTRO	50.4%	20.0%	28.6%
OWN ME ASTRO	81.2%	96.7%	88.2%

Table 10: Comparing CMP-LG and ASTRO directly on the basic annotation scheme

Table 10 compares the performance of our Naïve Bayes and Maximum Entropy classifiers on the two corpora for just the basic annotation scheme: Background, Own and Other. The features used are the set of Teufel features we have implemented (so it does not include unigram or bigram features).

The results show that classifiers for both corpora behave in quite similar ways on the basic scheme. Own is by far the most frequent category, and not surprisingly, it is most accurately classified in both domains. Background seems to be easier to distinguish in Astronomy, but Other is more distinct in Computational Linguistics.

Further, we see no advantage to using maximum entropy models over Naïve Bayes when the feature set is not sophisticated/overlapping enough, and the dataset large enough, to warrant the extra power (and cost).

6 Conclusion

This paper has presented new models of Argumentative Zoning using Maximum Entropy (ME) models. We have demonstrated that using ME models with standard word features, such as unigrams and bigrams, significantly outperforms Naïve Bayes models incorporating task-specific features. Further, these task-specific features had very little additional impact on the ME model.

Our ME model has raised the state-of-the-art in automatic Argumentative Zoning classification from 76% to 96.88% F-score on Teufel's Computational Linguistics conference paper corpus.

To test the wider applicability of Argumentative Zoning, we have annotated a corpus of Astronomy journal articles with a modified zone and content scheme, and achieved a similar level of performance using our maximum entropy classifier. We found that more sophisticated semantic features, e.g. gold-standard named entities, also had little impact on the accuracy of our classifier.

Now that we have a very accurate Argumentative Zone classifier, we would like to investigate the impact of Argumentative Zones in information retrieval, question answering, and summarization tasks, particularly in the astronomy domain, where we have additional tools such as the named entity recognizer.

In summary, using a maximum entropy classifier with simple unigram and bigram features results in a very accurate classifier for Argumentative Zones across multiple domains.

Acknowledgements

We would like to thank Sophie Liang and the anonymous reviewers for their helpful feedback on this paper. This work has been supported by the Australian Research Council under Discovery project DP0665973. The first author was supported by the Microsoft Research Asia Scholarship in IT at the University of Sydney.

References

arXiv. 2005. arxiv.org archive. `http://arxiv.org`.

R. Barzilay, K.R. McKeown, and M. Elhadad. 1999. Information fusion in the context of multi-document summarization. In *Proceedings of the 37th annual meeting of the Association for Computational Linguistics on Computational Linguistics*, pages 550–557. Association for Computational Linguistics Morristown, NJ, USA.

R. Brandow, K. Mitze, and L.F. Rau. 1995. Automatic condensation of electronic publications by sentence selection. *Information Processing and management*, 31(5):675–685.

A.L. Brown, J.D. Day, and R.S. Jones. 1983. The development of plans for summarizing texts. *Child Development*, pages 968–979.

Stanley Chen and Ronald Rosenfeld. 1999. A Gaussian prior for smoothing maximum entropy models. Technical report, Carnegie Mellon University, Pittsburgh, PA.

James R. Curran and Stephen Clark. 2003. Investigating GIS and smoothing for maximum entropy taggers. In *Proceedings of the 10th Conference of the European Chapter of the Association for Computational Linguistics*, pages 91–98, Budapest, Hungary, 12–17 April.

E. Frank, M.A. Hall, G. Holmes, R. Kirkby, B. Pfahringer, I.H. Witten, and L. Trigg. 2005. Weka-a machine learning workbench for data mining. *The Data Mining and Knowledge Discovery Handbook*, pages 1305–1314.

M. Johnson, S. Geman, S. Canon, Z. Chi, and S. Riezler. 1999. Estimators for stochastic 'unification-based' grammars. In *Proceedings of the 37th Meeting of the ACL*, pages 535–541, University of Maryland, MD.

W. Kintsch and T.A. Van Dijk. 1978. Toward a model of text comprehension and production. *Psychological review*, 85(5):363–94.

K. Knight and D. Marcu. 2000. Statistics-based summarization-step one: Sentence compression. In *Proceedings of the National Conference on Artificial Intelligence*, pages 703–710. Menlo Park, CA; Cambridge, MA; London; AAAI Press; MIT Press; 1999.

J. Kupiec, J. Pedersen, and F. Chen. 1995. A trainable document summarizer. In *Proceedings of the 18th annual international ACM SIGIR conference on Research and development in information retrieval*, pages 68–73. ACM New York, NY, USA.

M. Marcus, B. Santorini, and M. Marcinkiewicz. 1993. Building a large annotated corpus of english: The penn treebank.

T. Murphy, T. McIntosh, and J.R. Curran. 2006. Named entity recognition for astronomy literature. In *Proceedings of the 2006 Australasian Language Technology Workshop (ALTW)*.

K. Nigam, J. Lafferty, and A. McCallum. 1999. Using maximum entropy for text classification. In *Proceedings of the IJCAI-99 Workshop on Machine Learning for Information Filtering*, pages 61–67, Stockholm, Sweden.

Adwait Ratnaparkhi. 1996. A maximum entropy part-of-speech tagger. In *Proceedings of the EMNLP Conference*, pages 133–142, Philadelphia, PA.

J.C. Reynar and A. Ratnaparkhi. 1997. A maximum entropy approach to identifying sentence boundaries. In *Proceedings of the fifth conference on Applied natural language processing*, pages 16–19.

R. Rosenfeld. 1996. A maximum entropy approach to adaptive statistical language modeling. *Computer, Speech and Language*, 10:187–228.

J.M. Swales. 1990. *Genre analysis: English in academic and research settings.* Cambridge University Press.

S. Teufel and M. Moens. 2002. Summarising scientific articles — experiments with relevance and rhetorical status. *Computational Linguistics*, 28(4):409–445.

S. Teufel, J. Carletta, and M. Moens. 1999. An annotation scheme for discourse-level argumentation in research articles. In *Proceedings of EACL 1999.*

S. Teufel, A. Siddharthan, and D. Tidhar. 2006. Automatic classification of citation function. In *Proceedings of the 2006 Conference on Empirical Methods in Natural Language Processing*, pages 103–110.

S. Teufel. 1999. *Argumentative zoning: Information extraction from scientific text.* Ph.D. thesis, University of Edinburgh, Edinburgh, UK.

Classification of Research Papers into a Patent Classification System Using Two Translation Models

Hidetsugu Nanba
Hiroshima City University
3-4-1 Ozukahigashi, Hiroshima 731-3194 Japan
nanba@hiroshima-cu.ac.jp

Toshiyuki Takezawa
Hiroshima City University
3-4-1 Ozukahigashi, Hiroshima 731-3194 Japan
takezawa@hiroshima-cu.ac.jp

Abstract

Classifying research papers into patent classification systems enables an exhaustive and effective invalidity search, prior art search, and technical trend analysis. However, it is very costly to classify research papers manually. Therefore, we have studied automatic classification of research papers into a patent classification system. To classify research papers into patent classification systems, the differences in terms used in research papers and patents should be taken into account. This is because the terms used in patents are often more abstract or creative than those used in research papers in order to widen the scope of the claims. It is also necessary to do exhaustive searches and analyses that focus on classification of research papers written in various languages. To solve these problems, we propose some classification methods using two machine translation models. When translating English research papers into Japanese, the performance of a translation model for patents is inferior to that for research papers due to the differences in terms used in research papers and patents. However, the model for patents is thought to be useful for our task because translation results by patent translation models tend to contain more patent terms than those for research papers. To confirm the effectiveness of our methods, we conducted some experiments using the data of the Patent Mining Task in the NTCIR-7 Workshop. From the experimental results, we found that our method using translation models for both research papers and patents was more effective than using a single translation model.

1 Introduction

Classification of research papers into patent classification systems makes it possible to conduct an exhaustive and effective prior art search, invalidity search, and technical trend analysis. However, it would be too costly and time-consuming to have the research paper's authors or another professional classify such documents manually. Therefore, we have investigated the classification of research papers into a patent classification system.

In previous studies, classification of patents was conducted as subtasks in the 5th and 6th NTCIR workshops (Iwayama *et al.*, 2005; Iwayama *et al.*, 2007). In these subtasks, participants were asked to classify Japanese patents using the File Forming Term (F-term) system, which is a classification system for Japanese patents. Here, we have focused on the classification of research papers, and we need to take into account the differences in terms used in research papers and patents because the terms used in patents are often more abstract or creative than those used in research papers in order to widen the scope of the claims. For example, the scholarly term "machine translation" can be expressed as "automatic translation" or "language conversion" in patent documents. In addition to taking the differences of genres into account, it is necessary to do exhaustive searches and analyses focusing on the classification of research papers written in various languages.

To solve these problems, we propose some classification methods using two machine translation models. When translating English research papers into Japanese, the performance of a translation model for patents is generally inferior to that for research papers, because the terms used

Proceedings of the 2009 Workshop on Text and Citation Analysis for Scholarly Digital Libraries, ACL-IJCNLP 2009, pages 27–35,
Suntec, Singapore, 7 August 2009.

in patents are different from those in research papers. However, we thought that a translation model for patents might be useful for our task, because translation results using the patent translation model tend to contain more patent terms than those obtained using the model for research papers. In this paper, we confirm the effectiveness of our methods using the data of the Cross-genre Subtask (E2J) in the 7th NTCIR Workshop (NTCIR-7) Patent Mining Task (Nanba *et al.*, 2008:b).

The remainder of this paper is organized as follows. Section 2 describes related work. Section 3 describes our methods. To investigate the effectiveness of our methods, we conducted some experiments, and Section 4 reports the experimental results. We present some conclusions in Section 5.

2 Related Work

In this section, we describe some related studies on "cross-genre information access" and "cross-lingual information access".

Cross-genre Information Access

Much research has been done in the field of cross-genre information retrieval and document classification. The technical survey task in the NTCIR-3 workshop (Iwayama *et al.*, 2002) is an example. This task aimed to retrieve patents relevant to a given newspaper article. In this task, Itoh *et al.* (2002) focused on "Term Distillation". The distribution of the frequency of the occurrence of words was known to be different between newspaper articles and patents. For example, the word "president" often appears in newspaper articles, while this word seldom appears in patents. As a result, unimportant words such as "president" were assigned high scores in patents when using tf*idf to weight words. Term Distillation is a technique that can prevent such cases by filtering out words that can be assigned incorrect weights. This idea was also used to link news articles and blog entries (Ikeda *et al.*, 2006).

Another approach for cross-genre information retrieval was that used by Nanba *et al.* (2008:a), who proposed a method to integrate a research paper database and a patent database by analyzing citation relations between research papers and patents. For the integration, they extracted bibliographic information of cited literature in "prior art" fields in Japanese patent applications. Using this integrated database, users can retrieve patents that relate to a particular research paper by tracing citation relations between research papers and patents. However, the number of cited papers among patent applications is not sufficient to retrieve related papers or patents, even though the number of opportunities for citing papers in patents or for citing patents in papers has been increasing recently.

As another approach for cross-genre information retrieval, Nanba *et al.* (2009) proposed a method to paraphrase scholarly terms into patent terms (e.g., paraphrasing "floppy disc" into "magnetic recording medium"). They focused on citation relationships between research papers and patents for the paraphrased terms. Generally, a research paper and a patent that have a citation relationship tend to be in the same research field. Therefore, they paraphrased a scholarly term into a patent term in two steps: (1) retrieve research papers that contain a given scholarly term in their titles, and (2) extract patent terms from patents that have citation relations with the retrieved papers.

The NTCIR-7 Patent Mining Task (Nanba *et al.*, 2008:b) is another example of research done on information access using research papers and patents. The aim of the Patent Mining Task was to classify research papers written in either Japanese or English using the International Patent Classification (IPC) system, which is a global standard hierarchical patent classification system. The following four subtasks were included in this task, and 12 groups participated in three of them: Japanese, English, and Cross-lingual (J2E) subtasks.

- **Japanese subtask:** classification of Japanese research papers using patent data written in Japanese.
- **English subtask:** classification of English research papers using patent data written in English.
- **Cross-lingual subtask (J2E):** classification of Japanese research papers using patent data written in English.
- **Cross-lingual subtask (E2J):** classification of English research papers using patent data written in Japanese.

Because the number of categories (IPC codes) that research papers were classified into was very large (30,855), only two participating groups employed machine learning, which is the most standard approach in the NLP field. The other groups used the k-Nearest Neighbor (k-NN) method. Among all participant groups, only Mase and Iwayama's group (2008) coped with the problem of the differences in terms between research papers and patents. Mase and Iwayama used a pseudo-relevance feedback method to collect related patent terms for a given research paper. First, they retrieved patents relevant to a given research paper. Next, they extracted patent terms from the top n retrieved patents. Then they retrieved patents again using the patent terms extracted in the second step. Finally, they classified research papers using the k-NN method. However, they reported that a simple k-NN based method was superior to the method based on the pseudo-relevance feedback method. In this paper, we also examined our methods using the data of the NTCIR-7 Patent Mining Task.

TREC Chemistry Track[1] is another related study involving research papers and patents. This track aims for cross-genre information retrieval using research papers and patents in the chemical field. This track started in 2009 under the Text Retrieval Conference (TREC), and the details including experimental results will be reported at the final meeting to be held in November 2009.

Cross-lingual Information Access

Much research has been done on cross-lingual information access using research papers and patents. In the NTCIR workshop, cross-lingual information retrieval tasks have been carried out using research papers (Kando *et al.*, 1999; Kando *et al.*, 2001) and patents (Fujii *et al.*, 2004; Fujii *et al.*, 2005; Fujii *et al.*, 2007). In the CLEF evaluation workshop, the cross-lingual patent retrieval task "CLEF-IP" was initiated in 2009[2]. The cross-lingual subtask in the NTCIR-7 Patent Mining Task (Nanba *et al.*, 2008:b) is another cross-lingual information access study.

Here, we describe two methods used in the cross-lingual subtask (J2E) in the Patent Mining Task (Bian and Teng, 2008, Clinchant and Renders, 2008). Bian and Teng (2008) translated Japanese research papers into English using three online translation systems (Google, Excite, and Yahoo! Babel Fish), and classified them using a k-NN-based text classifier. Clinchant and Renders (2008) automatically obtained a Japanese-English bilingual dictionary from approximately 300,000 pairs of titles from Japanese and English research papers (Kando *et al.*, 1999) using Giza[3], a statistical machine translation toolkit. Then they classified papers using this dictionary and a k-NN-based document classifier. Bian and Clinchant also participated in an English subtask and obtained almost the same mean average precision (MAP) scores as those of the J2E subtask.

Although the direction of translation of our system is different from Bian and Clinchant, we also tried our methods using the data of the cross-lingual subtask (E2J). We utilized the Giza toolkit in the same way as Clinchant, but our approach was different from Clinchant, because we solved the problem of "differences of terms used in research papers and patents" by using two translation models obtained from both research papers and patents parallel corpora.

3 Classification of Research Papers into a Patent Classification System

3.1 Our Methods

We explain here the procedure of our cross-genre, cross-lingual document classification method depicted in Figure 1. The goal of our task is to classify document *I* written in language L1 in genre G1 into a classification system (categories) using documents written in language L2 in genre G2, and classification codes were manually annotated to each of these documents. Generally, three steps are required for cross-genre, cross-lingual document classification: (1) translate document *I* into Language L2 using a translation model for genre G1 (document *O* in Figure 1), (2) paraphrase terms in document *O* into terms in genre G2 (document *O'*), and (3) classify *O'* into a classification system. Here, if a translation model for genre G2 is available, steps (1) and (2) can be resolved using this translation model, because terms in the translation results using the model are more appropriate in genre G2. However, as it is assumed that the translation model translates documents in genre G2, the translation results might contain more mistranslations than the results obtained by a model for genre G1. We therefore combine translation results (*O*+*O'*) produced by translation models for genre G1 and for G2. These results can be expected to contain terms in genre G2 and to minimize the effects of mistranslation by using the translation model for genre G1.

---

[1] https://wiki.ir-facility.org/index.php/TREC_Chemistry_Track
[2] http://www.ir-facility.org/the_irf/current-projects/clef-ip09-track/
[3] http://www.fjoch.com/GIZA++.html

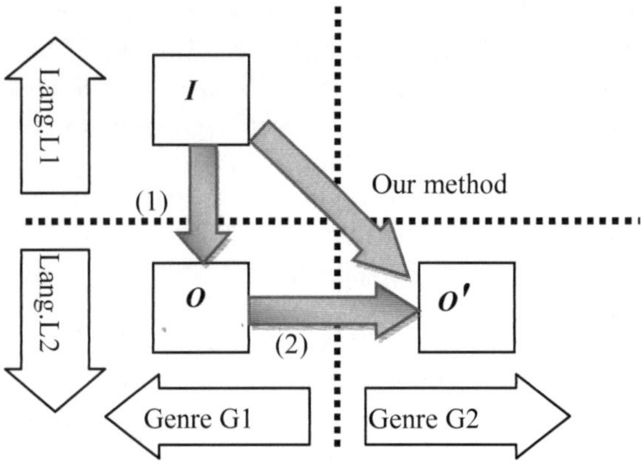

Figure 1: Overview of our method

3.2 System Configuration

The goal of our study is to classify English research papers (Language L1=English, Genre G1=research papers) into a patent classification using a patent data set written in Japanese (Language L2=Japanese, Genre G2=patents). Figure 2 shows the system configuration. Our system is comprised of a "Japanese index creating module" and a "document classification module". In the following, we explain both modules.

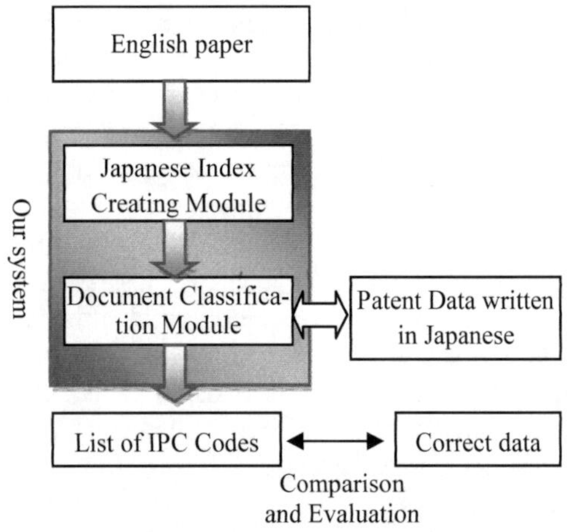

Figure 2: System configuration

Japanese Index Creating Module

When a title and abstract pair, as shown in Figure 3, is given, the module creates a Japanese index, shown in Figure 4[4], using translation models for research papers and for patents.

Here, the following two procedures (A) or (B) are possible for creating a Japanese index from an English paper: (A) translate the English title and abstract into Japanese; then create a Japanese index from them by extracting content terms[5], or (B) create an English index[6] from the English title and abstract, then translate each index term into Japanese. We conducted experiments using both procedures.

As translation tools, we used Giza and Moses[7]. We obtained translation models using a patent bilingual corpus containing 1,800,000 pairs of sentences (Fujii *et al.* 2008) and a research paper bilingual corpus containing 300,000 pairs automatically created from datasets of NTCIR-1 (Kando *et al.* 1999), and 2 (Kando *et al.* 2001) CLIR tasks.

Title: A Sandblast-Processed Color-PDP Phosphor Screen
Abstract: Barrier ribs in the color PDP have usually been fabricated by multiple screen printing. However, the precise rib printing of fine patterns for the high resolution display panel is difficult to make well in proportion as the panel size grow larger. On the other hand, luminance and luminous efficiency of reflective phosphor screen will be expected to increase when the phosphor is deposited on the inner wall of display cells. Sandblasting technique has been applied to make barrier ribs for the high resolution PDP and nonffat phosphor screens on the inner wall of display cells.

Figure 3: Example of an English title and abstract

18 形成 (formation)
18 ＰＤＰ (PDP)
18 型蛍光面 (type phosphor screen)
12 障壁形成 (barrier formation)
12 障壁 (barrier)
12 蛍光 (phosphor)
12 カラーＰＤＰ (color PDP)
12 反射型蛍光 (reflective phosphor)
12 型蛍光 (type phosphor)
12 サンドブラスト法 (Sandblasting technique)
9 サンドブラスト (Sandblasting)
(snip)

Figure 4: Example of a Japanese index

[4] Numerical values shown with index terms indicate term frequencies.

[5] As content terms, we extracted noun phrases (series of nouns), adjectives, and verbs using the Japanese morphological analyzer MeCab. (http://mecab.sourceforge.net)

[6] We used TreeTagger as a POS tagging tool. (http://www.ims.uni-stuttgart.de/projekte/corplex/TreeTagger/)

[7] http://www.statmt.org/moses/

We used two phrase tables for research papers and patents when translating English index terms into Japanese. For a given English term, we selected the Japanese term with the highest translation probability from the candidates in each table. These tables were automatically obtained in the process of constructing translation models for research papers and patents using Giza and Moses. However, there are several other ways to translate index terms, such as using bilingual dictionaries of technical terms or compositional semantics (Tonoike *et al.*, 2007), we employed a phrase table-based method because the effectiveness of this method was experimentally confirmed by Itakagi *et al.* (2007). In addition to this method, we also investigated using bilingual dictionaries of technical terms as baseline methods. Details of these methods are in Section 4.2.

Document Classification Module

We used Nanba's k-NN-based system (Nanba, 2008:c) for a Japanese subtask as a document classification module in our system. This module uses a patent retrieval engine (Nanba, 2007) which was developed for the NTCIR-6 Patent Retrieval Task (Fujii *et al.*, 2007). This engine introduced the Vector Space Model as a retrieval model, SMART (Salton, 1971) for term weighting, and noun phrases (sequence of nouns), verbs, and adjectives for index terms. The classification module obtained a list of IPC codes using the following procedure.

1. Retrieve top 170 results using the patent retrieval engine for a given research paper.
2. Extract IPC codes with relevance scores for the query from each retrieved patent in step 1.
3. Rank IPC codes using the following equation.

$$\text{Score}(X) = \sum_{i=1}^{n} \text{Relevance score of each patent}$$

Here, X and n indicate the IPC code and the number of patents that X was assigned to within the top 170 retrieved patents, respectively. Nanba determined the value of 170 using the dry run data and the training data of the NTCIR-7 Patent Mining Task.

3.3 Classification of Research Papers into International Patent Classification (IPC)

As a patent classification system for classification of research papers, we employed the International Patent Classification (IPC) system. The IPC system is a global standard hierarchical patent classification system. The sixth edition of the IPC contains more than 50,000 classes at the most detailed level[8]. The goal of our task was to assign one or more of these IPC codes at the most detailed level to a given research paper.

4 Experiments

To investigate the effectiveness of our method, we conducted some experiments. Section 4.1 describes the experimental procedure. Section 4.2 explains several methods that were compared in the experiments. Section 4.3 reports the experimental results, and Section 4.4 discusses them.

4.1 Experimental Method

We conducted some experiments using the data of the cross-lingual subtask (E2J) in the NTCIR-7 Patent Mining Task.

Correct data set

We used a data set for the formal run of the cross-lingual subtask in the NTCIR-7 Patent Mining Task (Nanba, *et al.*, 2008). In the data set, IPC codes were manually assigned to each 879 topics (research papers). For each topic, an average of 2.3 IPC codes was manually assigned. These correct data were compared with a list of IPC codes[9] by systems, and the systems were evaluated in terms of MAP (mean average precision). Here, the 879 topics were divided into two groups: group A, in which highly relevant IPC codes were assigned to 473 topics, and group B, in which relevant IPC codes were assigned to 406 topics. In our experiment, we evaluated several systems in two ways: using group A only and using both groups.

Document Sets

An overview of document sets used in our experiments is in Table 1. In the unexamined Japanese patent applications, manually assigned IPC codes are included together with full text patent data. These data were utilised to apply the k-NN method in our document classification module. NTCIR-1 and 2 CLIR Task test collections were used to obtain a translation model for research papers, which we mentioned in Section 3.2.

[8] Among 50,000 classes, 30,855 classes relevant to academic fields were used in the NTCIR-7 Patent Mining Task.

[9] The maximum number of IPC codes allowed to be output for a single topic was 1,000.

-

2002

Data	Year	Size	No.	Lang.
Unexamined Japanese patent applications	1993	100 GB	3.50 M	Japanese
NTCIR-1 and 2 CLIR Task	1988 - 1999	1.4 GB	0.26 M	Japanese /English

Table 1: Document sets

4.2 Alternatives

We conducted examinations using seven baseline methods, three proposed methods, and two upper-bound methods shown as follows. In the following, "SMT(X)" is a method to create a Japanese index after translating research papers using a translation model X. "Index(X)" is a method to create an English index, and to translate the index terms using a phrase table for translation model X.

Baseline methods

- SMT(Paper): Create a Japanese index after translating research papers using a translation model for research papers.
- SMT(Patent): Create a Japanese index after translating research papers using a model for patents.
- Index(Paper): First create an English index, then translate the index terms into Japanese using a phrase table for research papers.
- Index(Patent): First create an English index, then translate the index terms into Japanese using a phrase table for patents.
- SMT(Paper)+Hypernym: Paraphrase index terms created from "SMT(Paper)" by their hypernyms using a hypernym-hyponym thesaurus.
- Index(TechDic): Translate English index terms using a Japanese-English dictionary consisting of 450,000 technical terms[10].
- Index(EIJIRO): Translate English index terms using EIJIRO[11], a Japanese-English dictionary consisting of more than 1,000,000 pairs of terms.

Our methods

- Index(Paper)*Index(Patent): Product set of "Index(Paper)" and "Index(Patent)".
- Index(Paper)+Index(Patent): Union of "Index(Paper)" and "Index(Patent)".
- SMT(Paper)+Index(Patent): Union of "SMT(Paper)" and "Index(Patent)".

Upper-bound methods

- Japanese subtask: This is the same as the Japanese subtask in the NTCIR-7 Patent Mining Task. For this subtask, Japanese research papers, which are manual (ideal) translations of corresponding English papers, are input into a system.
- Japanese subtask+Index(Patent): Union of "Japanese subtask" and "Index(Patent)".

Another reason for using the baseline methods is that the terms used in patents are often more abstract or creative than those used in research papers, as mentioned in Section 1. Therefore, we paraphrased index terms in SMT(Paper) by their hypernyms using a hypernym/hyponym thesaurus (Nanba, 2007). Nanba automatically created this thesaurus consisting of 1,800,000 terms from 10 years of unexamined Japanese patent applications using a set of patterns, such as "NP_0 ya NP_1 nadono NP_2 (NP_2 such as NP_0 and NP_1)" (Hearst, 1992).

4.3 Experimental Results

Experimental results are given in Table 2. From the results, we can see that "SMT(Paper)" obtained the highest MAP scores when using topics in group A+B and in group A. Of the 10 methods used (except for the upper-bound methods), our method "SMT(Paper)+Index(Patent)" obtained the highest MAP score.

4.4 Discussion

Difference of terms between research and patents (Comparison of "Index(Paper)" and "Index(Patent)")

Although the quality of phrase tables for research papers ("Index(Paper)") and patents ("Index(Patent)") was not very different, the MAP score of "Index(Paper)" was 0.01 better than that of "Index(Patent)". To investigate this gap, we compared Japanese indices by "Index(Paper)" and "Index(Patent)". There were 69,100 English index terms in total, and 47,055 terms (47,055/69,100=0.681) were translated by the model for research papers, while 40,427 terms (40,427/69,100=0.585) were translated by the model for patents. Ten percent of this gap indicates that terms used in research papers and in patents are different, which causes the gap in MAP scores of "Index(Patent)" and "Index(Paper)".

[10] "Kagakugijutsu 45 mango taiyakujiten" Nichigai Associates, Inc., 2001.

[11] http://www.eijiro.jp/

Combination of "Index(Paper)" and "Index(Patent)"
When a term translated by the model for research papers matches a term translated by the model for patents, they seem to be a correct translation. Therefore, we examined "Index(Paper)*Index(Patent)". The method uses terms as an index when translation results by both models match. From the experimental results, this method obtained 0.1830 and 0.2230 of MAP scores when using topics in group A+B and in group A, respectively. These results indicate that the overlap of lexicons between research papers and patents is relatively large, and terms in this overlap are effective for our task. However, the MAP score of "Index(Paper)*Index(Patent)" was 0.02 lower than "Index(Paper)" and "Index(Patent)", which indicates that there are not enough terms in the overlap for our task.

In addition to "Index(Paper)*Index(Patent)", we also examined "Index(Paper)+Index(Patent)", which is a union of "Index(Paper)" and "Index(Patent)". From the experimental results, we obtained respective MAP scores of 0.2258 and 0.2596 when using topics in group A+B and in group A. These scores are 0.01 to 0.02 higher than the scores of "Index(Paper)" and "Index(Patent)". These encouraging results indicate that our method using two translation models is effective for a cross-genre document classification task.

Effectiveness of "SMT(Paper)+Index(Patent)"
In addition to "Index(Paper)", "SMT(Paper)" also obtained high MAP scores. Therefore, we combined "Index(Patent)" with "SMT(Paper)" instead of "Index(Paper)". From the experimental results, we found that this approach ("SMT(Paper)+Index(Patent)") produced MAP scores of 0.2633 when using topics in group A+B and 0.2807 when using topics in group A. These scores were the highest of all, almost approaching the results of upper-bound methods.

Comparison of "Index(TechDic)", "Index(EIJIRO)", "Index(Paper)", and "Index(Patent)"
Both "Index(TechDic)" and "Index(EIJIRO)" were worse than "Index(Paper)" and "Index(Patent)" by more than 0.05 in the MAP scores. These results were due to the lower number of terms translated by each method. Because phrase tables for research papers and patents were automatically created, they were not as correct as "TechDic" and "EIJIRO". However, the phrase tables were able to translate more English terms into Japanese in comparison with "TechDic" (30,008/69,100=0.434) and "EIJIRO" (37607/69,100=0.544), and these induced the difference of MAP scores.

Comparison of "SMT(Paper)+Hypernym" and "SMT(Paper)"
"SMT(Paper)+Hypernym" impaired "SMT(Paper)", because the method paraphrased unnecessary terms into their hypernyms. As a result, irrelevant patents were contained within the top 170 search results, and the k-NN method ranked irrelevant IPC codes at higher levels. Our methods using two translation models are different from "SMT(Paper)+Hypernym" in this point because two translation models translate into the same term when a scholarly term need not be paraphrased.

Classification of Japanese research papers using "Index(Patent)"
As we mentioned above, the "Index(Paper)+Index(Patent)" and "SMT(Paper)+Index(Patent)" models improved the MAP scores of both "Index(Paper)" and "SMT(Paper)". We further investigated whether "Index(Patent)" could also improve monolingual document classification ("Japanese subtask+Index(Patent)"). In this method, a Japanese index was created from a manually written Japanese research paper, and this was combined with "Index(Patent)". The results showed that "Japanese subtask+Index(Patent)" could slightly improve MAP scores when using topics in group A+B and in group A.

Practicality of our method
Recall values for the top n results by "SMT(Paper)+Index(Patent)", which obtained the highest MAP score, are in Table 3. In this table, the results using all topics (group A+B) and the topics in group A are shown. The results indicate that almost 40% of the IPC codes were found within top 10 results, and 70% were found within the top 100. For practical use, we need to improve recall at the top 1, but we still believe that these results are useful for supporting beginners in patent searches. It is often necessary for searchers to use patent classification codes for effective patent retrieval, but professional skill and much experience are required to select relevant IPC codes. In such cases, our method is useful to look for relevant IPC codes.

	Method	group A+B	group A
Our methods	Index(Paper)*Index(Patent)	0.1830	0.2230
	Index(Paper)+Index(Patent)	0.2258	0.2596
	SMT(Paper)+Index(Patent)	**0.2633**	**0.2897**
Baseline methods	SMT(Paper)	0.2518	0.2777
	SMT(Patent)	0.2214	0.2507
	Index(Paper)	0.2169	0.2433
	Index(Patent)	0.2000	0.2373
	SMT(Paper)+Hypernym	0.2451	0.2647
	Index(TechDic)	0.1575	0.1773
	Index(EIJIRO)	0.1347	0.1347
Upper-bound	Japanese subtask	0.2958	0.3267
	Japanese subtask+Index(Patent)	0.3001	0.3277

Table 2: Evaluation results

5 Conclusion

We proposed several methods that automatically classify research papers into the IPC system using two translation models. To confirm the effectiveness of our method, we conducted some examinations using the data of the NTCIR-7 Patent Mining Task. The results showed that one of our methods "SMT(Paper)+Index(Patent)" obtained a MAP score of 0.2897. This score was higher than that of "SMT(Paper)", which used translation results by the translation model for research papers, and this indicates that our method is effective for cross-genre, cross-lingual document classification.

rank	group A	group A+B
1	0.117 (131/1115)	0.110 (226/2051)
2	0.186 (207/1115)	0.169 (347/2051)
3	0.239 (267/1115)	0.215 (440/2051)
4	0.278 (310/1115)	0.250 (512/2051)
5	0.311 (347/1115)	0.277 (567/2051)
10	0.420 (468/1115)	0.377 (774/2051)
20	0.524 (584/1115)	0.467 (958/2051)
50	0.659 (735/1115)	0.597 (1224/2051)
100	0.733 (817/1115)	0.673 (1381/2051)
500	0.775 (864/1115)	0.728 (1494/2051)
1000	0.775 (864/1115)	0.728 (1494/2051)

Table 3: Recall for top n results (SMT(Paper)+Index(Patent))

References

Guo-Wei Bian and Shun-Yuan Teng. 2008. Integrating Query Translation and Text Classification in a Cross-Language Patent Access System, *Proceeding of the 7th NTCIR Workshop Meeting*: 341-346.

Stephane Clinchant and Jean-Michel Renders. 2008. XRCE's Participation to Patent Mining Task at NTCIR-7, *Proceedings of the 7th NTCIR Workshop Meeting*: 351-353.

Atsushi Fujii, Makoto Iwayama, and Noriko Kando. 2004. Overview of Patent Retrieval Task at NTCIR-4, *Working Notes of the 4th NTCIR Workshop*: 225-232.

Atsushi Fujii, Makoto Iwayama, and Noriko Kando. 2005. Overview of Patent Retrieval Task at NTCIR-5, *Proceedings of the 5th NTCIR Workshop Meeting*: 269-277.

Atsushi Fujii, Makoto Iwayama, and Noriko Kando. 2007. Overview of the Patent Retrieval Task at NTCIR-6 Workshop, *Proceedings of the 6th NTCIR Workshop Meeting*: 359-365.

Atsushi Fujii, Masao Utiyama, Mikio Yamamoto, and Takehito Utsuro. 2008. Overview of the Patent Translation Task at the NTCIR-7 Workshop, *Proceedings of the 7th NTCIR Workshop Meeting*: 389-400.

Marti A. Hearst. 1992. Automatic Acquisition of Hyponyms from Large Text Corpora, *Proceedings of the 14th International Conference on Computational Linguistics*: 539-545.

Daisuke Ikeda, Toshiaki Fujiki, and Manabu Okumura. 2006. Automatically Linking News Articles to Blog Entries, *Proceedings of AAAI Spring Symposium Series Computational Approaches to Analyzing Weblogs*: 78-82.

Masaki Itagaki, Takako Aikawa, and Xiaodong He. 2007. Automatic Validation of Terminology Translation Consistency with Statistical Method, *Proceedings of MT summit XI*: 269-274.

Hideo Itoh, Hiroko Mano, and Yasushi Ogawa. 2002. Term Distillation for Cross-db Retrieval, *Working Notes of the 3rd NTCIR Workshop Meeting, Part III: Patent Retrieval Task*: 11-14.

Makoto Iwayama, Atsushi, Fujii, Noriko Kando, and Akihiko Takano. 2002. Overview of Patent Retrieval Task at NTCIR-3, *Working Notes of the 3rd NTCIR Workshop Meeting, Part III: Patent Retrieval Task*: 1-10.

Makoto Iwayama, Atsushi Fujii, and Noriko Kando. 2005. Overview of Classification Subtask at NTCIR-5 Patent Retrieval Task, *Proceedings of the 5th NTCIR Workshop Meeting*: 278-286.

Makoto Iwayama, Atsushi Fujii, and Noriko Kando. 2007. Overview of Classification Subtask at NTCIR-6 Patent Retrieval Task, *Proceedings of the 6th NTCIR Workshop Meeting*: 366-372.

Noriko Kando, Kazuko Kuriyama, Toshihiko Nozue, Koji Eguchi, Hiroyuki Kato, and Soichiro Hidaka. 1999. Overview of IR Tasks at the first NTCIR Workshop, *Proceedings of the 1st NTCIR Workshop on Research in Japanese Text Retrieval and Term Recognition*: 11-44.

Noriko Kando, Kazuko Kuriyama, and Makoto Yoshioka. 2001. Overview of Japanese and English Information Retrieval Tasks (JEIR) at the Second NTCIR Workshop, *Proceedings of the 2nd NTCIR Workshop Meeting*: 4-37 - 4-60.

Hisao Mase and Makoto Iwayama. 2008. NTCIR-7 Patent Mining Experiments at Hitachi, *Proceedings of the 7th NTCIR Workshop Meeting*: 365-368.

Hidetsugu Nanba. 2007. Query Expansion using an Automatically Constructed Thesaurus, *Proceedings of the 6th NTCIR Workshop Meeting*: 414-419.

Hidetsugu Nanba, Natsumi Anzen, and Manabu Okumura:a. 2008. Automatic Extraction of Citation Information in Japanese Patent Applications, *International Journal on Digital Libraries*, 9(2): 151-161.

Hidetsugu Nanba, Atsushi Fujii, Makoto Iwayama, and Taiichi Hashimoto:b. 2008. Overview of the Patent Mining Task at the NTCIR-7 Workshop, *Proceedings of the 7th NTCIR Workshop Meeting*: 325-332.

Hidetsugu Nanba:c. 2008. Hiroshima City University at NTCIR-7 Patent Mining Task. *Proceedings of the 7th NTCIR Workshop Meeting*: 369-372.

Hidetsugu Nanba, Hideaki Kamaya, Toshiyuki Takezawa, Manabu Okumura, Akihiro Shinmori, and Hidekazu Tanigawa. 2009. Automatic Translation of Scholarly Terms into Patent Terms, *Journal of Information Processing Society Japan TOD*, 2(1): 81-92. (in Japanese)

Gerald Salton. 1971. *The SMART Retrieval System - Experiments in Automatic Document Processing.* Prentice-Hall, Inc., Upper Saddle River, NJ.

Masatsugu Tonoike. Mitsuhiro Kida, Toshihiro Takagi, Yasuhiro Sakai, Takehito Utsuro, and Satoshi Sato. 2005. Translation Estimation for Technical Terms using Corpus Collected from the Web, *Proceedings of the Pacific Association for Computational Linguistics*: 325-331.

Detecting key sentences for automatic assistance in peer reviewing research articles in educational sciences

Ágnes Sándor
Xerox Research Centre Europe
6. ch. Maupertuis 38240 Meylan, France
A.Sandor@xrce.xerox.com

Angela Vorndran
DIPF
Schlossstrasse 29, 60486 Frankfurt, Germany
vorndran@dipf.de

Abstract

The evaluation of scientific performance is gaining importance in all research disciplines. The basic process of the evaluation is peer reviewing, which is a time-consuming activity. In order to facilitate and speed up peer reviewing processes we have developed an exploratory NLP system in the field of educational sciences. The system highlights key sentences, which are supposed to reflect the most important threads of the article The highlighted sentences offer guidance on the content-level while structural elements – the title, abstract, keywords, section headings – give an orientation about the design of the argumentation in the article. The system is implemented using a discourse analysis module called concept matching applied on top of the Xerox Incremental Parser, a rule-based dependency parser. The first results are promising and indicate the directions for the future development of the system.

1 Introduction

With the increase of centrally allocated research funding, the growing number of conferences, workshops and journals, the evaluation of scientific articles has become a central problem of the scientific community (see for example Whitley and Gläser, 2007). The evaluation of articles consists in peer reviewing, i.e. peers' reading, understanding and commenting the articles. The peer reviewing process is a matter of extensive research (e.g. Bornmann 2003, Lu 2005, 2008) discussing its reliability and evaluation methods.

Peer reviewing is a very time-consuming assignment, and Natural Language Processing (NLP) technologies might provide tools that could shorten the time that peer reviewers take to process the articles.

Within the 7th framework EU project, European Educational Research Quality Indicators (http://www.eerqi.eu), we have set up this goal, and are developing a tool for providing assistance to peer reviewers in educational sciences. We do not know of any other work with this perspective.

Our approach consists in highlighting key sentences in the articles that can be regarded as the logical backbone of the article. Our tool does not evaluate, but aims at focusing the evaluator's attention on the parts of the texts that are relevant as a basis for his/her judgment. Nor does this tool check if the texts conform to some formal norms of scientific writing.

We regard highlighting key sentences as a complement to the processing guidance that the structural layout of the articles provides. The structural layout of scientific articles – title, abstract, keywords, section headings – guide the reader in processing the logical, argumentative and content-wise development of the article at different levels: The title is the brief indication of the topic, the keywords yield the conceptual context of the topic, the abstract provides a concise summary of the problems and results, and the section headings guide the reader step by step in the development of the article. Besides these waymarkers, the highlighted key sentences are meant to be an intermediary representation of content development between the title, the keywords, the abstract and the section headings on the one hand and the whole article on the other hand.

Since we define key sentences as those sentences that sum up the main messages of the articles, and since peer reviewing consists in judging the scientific value of the main messages, we

Proceedings of the 2009 Workshop on Text and Citation Analysis for Scholarly Digital Libraries, ACL-IJCNLP 2009, pages 36–44, Suntec, Singapore, 7 August 2009.

assume that highlighting key sentences both helps understanding and provides evidence for the peer reviewer's evaluation. By highlighting we intend to add a relevant and coherent dimension of the representation of the flow of the article, which is otherwise hidden, and which the reader has to discover in order to understand the article.

Highlighting is carried out using the Xerox Incremental Parser (XIP), a rule-based dependency parser (Ait-Mokhtar et al., 2002).

We will first provide a brief review of related work. This is followed by the description of the role of structural layout in educational research articles, which we wish to complement by highlighting sentences. In the subsequent sections we define the attributes of key sentences that serve as a basis for their detection and describe the natural language processing system. In the succeeding section we present our first tests for validating our approach, and finally we draw some conclusions and indicate the directions in which we plan to carry on this work.

2 Related work

Our work is in line with the growing amount of research in documentation sciences and natural language processing that takes into account the argumentative structure of research articles in tasks such as information retrieval, information extraction, navigation within documents and summarization.

In the domain of information retrieval as far back as the beginning of the 1990's Liddy (1991) claimed that additional functions for search instruments could benefit from including the discourse-level context of the retrieved search terms in the interpretation of the results. Liddy stressed the "semantic roles" of concepts in a document as opposed to the simple occurrence of search terms. Oddy et al. (1992) proceed in this line of research and state that discourse-level structures in research texts could be useful to support retrieval for the user because they represent structural qualities recognized by the reader independent of the topic of the research. Both concentrate on the analysis of abstracts of research articles and propose a system to combine topical with structural information in the retrieval process.

Kando (1997) also emphasizes the importance of the discourse-level context of search terms in the retrieved documents. The allocation of retrieved passages to functional units and thus the possibility to gain information about article structures provides a valuable opportunity to improve the user's assessment of the retrieved documents. A similar method of annotating text passages according to their function in the text is conducted by Mizuta et al. (2006) with the objective of categorizing articles in different document genres.

Teufel and Moens (2002) base automatic summarization on extracting sentences annotated with respect to their discourse function in the text.

Lisacek et al (2005) detect sentences in biomedical articles that describe substantially new research based on analyzing discourse functions.

Another line of research to exploit the argumentative structure for navigation and information extraction is inspired by the semantic web. Instead of automatically discovering argument structures in texts, the approach aims at creating conceptually motivated processing editors in which the users insert content according to its argumentative function. (see for example Uren et al., 2007, Couto and Minel, 2007.)

3 The structure of educational research articles

Research articles in the educational sciences tend to display a very heterogeneous structure, like articles in many other fields in social sciences and humanities. While the thematic contents of the articles are structured according to the requirements of the topic, frequent occurrences of a unifying structure are introductory and concluding chapters. However, where these chapters appear they do not display uniform headings (cf. Fiedler, 1991:98). Likewise Ruiying and Allison (2004) show, for example, that the structure of research articles in linguistics is does not conform to a common model, and section headings in many cases do not refer to the function of the chapter but to the thematic contents. Brett (1994) and Holmes (1997) observe basic structural features in the articles in political sciences and sociology. They state, however, that the section headings are usually not standardized.

In contrast to the heterogeneity of the structure and section headings of research articles in social sciences and humanities those in the hard sciences show a relatively uniform structure, and often follow the well-known pattern of Introduction – Methods – Results – Discussion, which renders their reading easier.

The structural heterogeneity of social science and humanities research articles, and particularly those within educational sciences, derives from the coverage of a wide range of research problems and the consequential variation the methods applied. This discipline includes theoretically embedded discussions as well as empirical studies or material for school praxis. These differences in the referenced subjects are reflected in the way the research articles are organized and presented. Montesi and Owen (2008:151) notice a high grade of liberty granted by the educational sciences journals for the presentation of submitted papers. They also describe a clear distinction between qualitative and quantitative approaches in research articles, the latter displaying a closer connection in structural aspects to the exact sciences than the former.

In the framework of this study we compared the structural properties of fifteen articles from three journals: the British Journal of Educational Studies (BJES), the Educational Psychology Review (EPR) and the International Journal of Educational Research (IJER). These are educational research journals covering a wide variety of topics from educational psychology to school instruction. We have made the following observations:

a) Some section headings follow the functional structuring of natural science articles, some do not. About half of the articles contain an 'Introduction' and/or a 'Conclusion', one third has a 'Methods' section and 26% of the articles has a section entitled 'Results', 'Findings' or 'Conclusion'. Thus a basis for a functionally orientated article structure can be perceived in the first and last chapters of most of the articles. Nearly 60% of the section headings, however, are oriented towards aspects of the content of the articles and show no predefined form.

b) All of the articles are preceded by an abstract and eleven of them have keywords assigned to them.

   The keywords play an important role in our highlighting approach, since they are supposed to convey the basis for topical relevance. The number of keywords assigned per article is between two and nine. While some keywords are applied only a few times in the article, others are used 60 or even over 100 times. In some cases the keywords are very common words ('teachers', 'education') and they are used frequently throughout the text. In these cases the highlighted sentences are supposed to indicate relevant, terminological uses of those common, non-specialised words. In other cases the keywords are rare, but they are terms used in reduced contexts, for example, terminological expressions related to the field of research. Those are very useful for a quick overview over the research topic. Keywords appearing very rarely or not at all often belong to a more general level of terminology.

   From an information extraction point of view the importance of the terms in the thread of the article is known to be related to their places of occurrence: in the title, the abstract, the section headings or even in the titles of the bibliography terms have more significance than in the rest of the article. This property of terms is used in search options in digital libraries. An appearance of the query term in the introduction or conclusion could also be a hint for the term being relevant for the scientific context or the results of the study whereas terms referring to the methodology or rather non-specific terms do not convey much information about the central contents of the text.

c) The abstract is supposed to sum up the most important aspects of a research article. The articles analyzed show that in general the sentences in the abstract correspond to assertions made throughout the articles in most of the different sections. In a few cases most sentences of the abstract were also taken up in the introductory or concluding part of the article with a summarizing function.

In this section we have shown that owing to the large number of research fields in educational sciences there is a high variety in the structural design and organisation of the contents of educational science research articles. In contrast to research literature in the natural sciences, the understanding of educational sciences articles is not promoted by predefined structuring of the contents. Additionally, a terminological vagueness sometimes stands in the way of using keywords as reliable content indicators. In our approach we therefore aim at a representation of article contents independent of the structural properties of the articles.

4 The detection of key sentences

In defining the characteristic features of key sentences that serve as a basis for their detection we rely on the kinds of judgments peer review evaluations are supposed to make (Bridges 2008).[1] We have summed up these judgments as follows: the relevance of the topic, the clarity of the problem statement, the coherence of the argumentation and the well-foundedness of the conclusions. These criteria of judgment are often presented as questions in the evaluation forms that peer reviewers are asked to fill in. Based on these evaluation criteria we define key sentences as sentences that describe research problems, purposes and conclusions related to the topic of the articles as indicated by the keywords.

The key sentences receive two types of labels in our system: SUMMARY – the sentences that convey either the goal or the conclusion - or PROBLEM – the sentences that mention research problems. Some sentences get both labels. Labeling is carried out by rules, which rely on the conceptual definition of SUMMARY and PROBLEM sentences as we show below.

In order to explain the conceptual definition we present a series of examples. The following SUMMARY and PROBLEM sentences are the first and last three key sentences detected in the same article (Barrow, 2008). In the first series of examples the keywords are underlined:

Beginning:

(1) PROBLEM: The most challenging questions concern whether the body provides an alternative route to knowledge, if so of what.

(2) PROBLEM_SUMMARY I do not question this belief, but in this paper I shall try to differentiate between and evaluate a number of quite distinct claims about the importance of the body in relation to schooling in general and education in particular.

(3) PROBLEM: However, to assume, as some philosophers would, that acceptance of that premise concludes the debate on the question of education and the body, by implicitly claiming that education has nothing to do with the body per se, would be absurd.

End:

(4) SUMMARY: Do I therefore conclude, as rationalist philosophers of education are generally supposed to conclude, that education has nothing to do with the body?

(5) PROBLEM: Second, while most of the claims made about the body and knowledge are variously opaque, suspect, or clearly wrong, it remains true that to be fully aware of or to fully understand an art form such as ballet, you need to engage in it.

(6) PROBLEM: More generally, let us attempt to articulate more straightforward arguments for the inclusion of sports and other forms of bodily activity in the school curriculum than obscure and unconvincing claims to the effect that they are necessary, sufficient or even directly relevant to well-developed and well-rounded educational understanding.

It is apparent from these sentences that approaching the task by providing a normalized factual extraction related to the keywords as in traditional information extraction would be both very problematic - even in an intellectual (as opposed to automatic) way - and may also be useless in the case of an article whose discipline is not related to describing facts, but rather to arguing about concepts. On the other hand, the human reader clearly seizes that these sentences do describe problems, aims and conclusions related to the underlined keywords.[2] In the next step we define the characteristic features of SUMMARY and PROBLEM sentences as being conveyed independently of the factual propositions.

The features of the key sentences are assigned by applying the concept-matching framework described in the following series of examples. This framework had previously been successfully used in revealing argumentative functions of research articles in a text-mining application of biomedical abstracts (Lisacek et al., 2005) and in citation-type analysis (Sándor et al., 2006). (Besides processing scientific articles, concept matching has also been used in risk detection in Sándor, 2009.)

The features of key sentences are determined by the argumentative expressions in the sentences, which in some way comment on the core factual propositions. In the next series of examples we have underlined these argumentative expressions in the same set of sentences:

[1] In a preliminary experiment we tried to identify key sentences in an example-based way. Six scholars marked the key sentences in four articles from four domains according to the same evaluation criteria. There were hardly any overlaps. This led us to define key sentences.

[2] At this point we do not attempt to specify the kind of relationship between the argument types and the keywords: this relationship remains simple co-occurrence.

Beginning:

(1) PROBLEM: The most challenging questions concern whether the body provides an alternative route to knowledge, if so of what.

(2) PROBLEM_SUMMARY I do not question this belief, but in this paper I shall try to differentiate between and evaluate a number of quite distinct claims about the importance of the body in relation to schooling in general and education in particular.

(3) PROBLEM: However to assume, as some philosophers would, that acceptance of that premise concludes the debate on the question of education and the body, by implicitly claiming that education has nothing to do with the body per se, would be absurd.

End:

(4) SUMMARY: Do I therefore conclude, as rationalist philosophers of education are generally supposed to conclude, that education has nothing to do with the body?

(5) PROBLEM: Second, while most of the claims made about the body and knowledge are variously opaque, suspect, or clearly wrong, it remains true that to be fully aware of or to fully understand an art form such as ballet, you need to engage in it.

(6) PROBLEM: More generally, let us attempt to articulate more straightforward arguments for the inclusion of sports and other forms of bodily activity in the school curriculum than obscure and unconvincing claims to the effect that they are necessary, sufficient or even directly relevant to well-developed and well- rounded educational understanding.

The detection is based on the words underlined. The system recognizes them since they belong to a database of previously compiled sets of words. The sets correspond to more or less loosely understood semantic fields that have been found to be relevant in scholarly argumentation in the previous applications of the concept-matching framework. The compilation of the lists has been entirely manual. Starting from a small number of seed words we incrementally extend the list over subsequent analyses and testing. Having worked out a first concept-matching system, its modification for a new scholarly domain takes some weeks provided that a sufficiently large corpus is available. We are carrying out experiments for automatic enrichment with the help of Wordnet, but the results have not been satisfactory up to this point. However, since the semantic fields concerned contain a relatively well-identifiable vocabulary within the genre of scholarly writing, most of these words can be obtained from textbooks on academic writing.

In the concept-matching framework these sets of words and expressions are called constituent concepts. In previous applications nine constituent concepts have been identified for labeling argumentative sentences (Sándor, 2007). Out of these we use five here: MENTAL, IDEA, PUBLICATION, DEICTIC, CONTRAST.

In the present system we have used all the words that have been compiled for labeling argumentative functions of biomedical research abstracts, and we have added a few others after having studied some educational research articles. Augmenting the list of words in the constituent concepts undoubtedly increases the coverage of the system, although we have found that the words already compiled yield fairly large coverage.

In terms of the constituent concepts we define PROBLEMs as CONTRASTed IDEAs or CONTRASTs in MENTAL operations involved in research, while SUMMARIES of one's research goals and conclusions consist in pointing out in the current (DEICTIC) PUBLICATION one's (DEICTIC) IDEAs or MENTAL operations. We cite now the example sentences only through the constituent concepts of PROBLEM and SUMMARY:

Beginning:

(1) PROBLEM: ... challenging[C,M] questions[C,M] ... whether[C] ... alternative[C] ... to knowledge[I] ...

(2) PROBLEM_SUMMARY: I[D] ... question[C,M] this belief[M] ... in this[D] paper[P]...

(3) PROBLEM: However[C] to assume[C,M], ... that acceptance[MC] ... concludes[C,M] the debate[C,I] ..., by ... claiming[C,M] ... would be absurd[C].

End:

(4) SUMMARY: ...I[D] ... conclude[C,M] ...

(5) PROBLEM: ... while[C] ... the claims[I] ... are ... wrong[C] ...

(6) PROBLEM: ... unconvincing[C,M] claims[I] ...

It is apparent that the words that represent the constituent concepts in these sentential skeletons constitute purely argumentative expressions and are void of any factual proposition.

However, not all sentences containing these words convey the target concepts. Consider for example the following sentence from a research article (Meinberg and Stern, 2003.):

(7) Only 1.8% of the claims were attributed to wrong-site surgery, but 84% of the claims due to wrong-site surgery resulted in payment to the plaintiff compared ...

In order to differentiate between relevant and irrelevant ways of combining the constituent concepts in a sentence our framework proposes syntactic criteria: sentences are labeled in case the constituent concepts are in syntactic dependency relationship with each other. The kind of syntactic relationship is not specified.

The restriction of syntactic dependencies is especially relevant in the case when the constituent concepts are function words (like e.g. *not*) or have a general sense (like e.g. *work*). At this point we have not measured the impact of this restriction on recall and precision.

We have built the concept-matching grammar for labeling argumentation types on top of a general-purpose dependency grammar developed in XIP. In the concept-matching grammar we define the argumentative expressions as those syntactic dependencies where both words belong to the particular concepts that constitute the target concepts as defined above. The only exceptions to the syntactic constraint are sentential adverbs (like "however"), for which the XIP grammar does not extract any syntactic dependencies. The highlighted sentences are those that contain the labeled argumentative expressions.

5 First tests

Our exploratory system is based on several consecutive hypotheses, the validity of which should be tested incrementally.

The first hypothesis is that the key sentences relevant for peer reviewing are those that describe the problems, aims and results in the articles, and that these sentences contain the keywords provided with the articles. The second hypothesis is that these sentences can be detected using the concept-matching grammar. Finally the third hypothesis is that highlighting these sentences can save peer reviewers' time evaluating articles.

Owing to the complexity and relative vagueness of the task, we have not been able to set up either a formal or a statistically significant evaluation up to now. For this article we have carried out an initial internal test[3] towards the validation of the first two hypotheses.

In a test corpus of five articles from the three educational research journals mentioned in Section 3 (BJES, EPR, IJES) we checked if the sentences highlighted by the system convey relevant information in the argumentative development of the paper and if we find other key sentences that are not highlighted. Next we analyzed the causes of silence and noise in order to evaluate our basic assumptions.

Table 1 summarizes the results of the test over the five articles in terms of recall and precision of the key sentences, and also indicates the percentage of key sentences out of all the sentences in the articles. Recall is defined as the number of correct sentences highlighted divided by the total number of sentences that we considered to be key sentences. Precision is defined as the number of correct sentences highlighted divided by the total number of sentences highlighted.

Table 2 shows if the missing sentences identified as key sentences by the evaluator contain keywords or not. It also displays the number of missing sentences in each article by type of error. Table 3 shows the number of false positive sentences according to the types of the causes of the error.

Article	Recall	Precision	Key sentences (Number of sentences)
BJES-1	77%	67%	17% (195)
BJES-2	69%	77%	11% (240)
EPR-1	39%	59%	8% (331)
EPR-2	30%	100%	3% (330)
IJER-1	35%	67%	2% (526)

Table 1. Recall and precision of key sentences detected and percentage of key sentences out of all the sentences in the article

[3] This test was carried out by one of the co-authors of this article who did not take part in the development of the NLP system.

Article	Keywords in sentence yes	no	1	2	3
BJES-1	6	1	4	2	3
BJES-2	5	1	1	-	5
EPR-1	13	12	3	6	16
EPR-2	13	10	-	-	23
IJER-1	8	3	-	1	10
All	45	27	8	9	57

Table 2. Causes of silence: 1.Incorrect analysis by the parser; 2.Inadequacy of the framework for the task; 3. Not SUMMARY or PROBLEM sentence according to our definition

Article	1	2	3
BJES-1	6	1	3
BJES-2	1	2	4
EPR-1	6	-	5
EPR-2	-	-	-
IJER-1	1	-	2
All	14	3	14

Table 3. Causes of noise: 1.The sentence matches the rules but is not important enough; 2.Incorrect analysis by the parser 3.Inadequacy of the framework for the task

We can observe significant differences according to the journals with respect to both hypotheses that we have tested. The three journals deal with rather different research topics ranging from theoretical discussions to empirical studies of students´ behavior. According to our results the important passages of these articles are characterized by different attributes: while in empirical studies more or less definite results can be presented, theoretical discussions rest more on a discursive level offering less clear conclusions to be identified as SUMMARY or PROBLEM sentences. This is reflected on the one hand in the differences in recall and precision among the journals and on the other hand in the differences in the number of sentences missing due to error-type 3 in Table 2.

In the EPR and in the IJER we found more key sentences that are neither SUMMARY nor PROBLEM sentences according to our definition than in the BJES. Most of these sentences convey definitions related to the key concept. Thus our first hypothesis seems to hold more for empirical studies than for theoretical ones. In order to increase the coverage of key sentences the system should be completed so that it also detects definitions, especially in the case of theoretical articles.

As for the presence of keywords in the key sentences, our results show that this is a relevant condition, however not necessary since a number of key sentences identified do not contain keywords. Further study is needed to identify the characteristic features of key sentences without keywords. We have carried out an additional test to see if the correct key sentences cover all the keywords in the list. In the five articles we have only found one keyword that was not present in any of the key sentences, but this word appeared only once in the whole article. The fact that relatively few sentences are detected in the articles and that in these sentences all the keywords are covered supports the hypothesis that the key sentences do play an important role in the thread of the article.

Among the errors leading to both silence and noise we have found a number of cases where the concept-matching framework in its present form is not convenient for the task of detecting key sentences that satisfy the conditions or filtering erroneous sentences. The reason for this in both cases is that the unit of concept-matching is the sentence, whereas in these cases a single sentence does not provide enough context for identifying or for specifying the target concepts respectively. Since the number of errors due to this reason is not very high we do not consider that these results invalidate the second hypothesis. The number of such false positives is quite significant, however, which might be disturbing for the user of the system. This kind of error could be overcome by enlarging the scope of concept-matching beyond the sentence. In this way we could filter out these false positives.

In a significant number of cases noise is not due to an error in the system but to the fact that the sentence is not important enough with respect to the development of the whole article. Whether this kind of noise is a significant disturbing factor for the user is to be tested in subsequent evaluation by users.

Finally, we have found few errors due to bugs in the grammar, which indicates that the recognition of SUMMARY and PROBLEM sentences is relatively reliable. These results also contribute to suggesting that the second hypothesis seems to hold.

6 Conclusion

In this article we have presented an exploratory system for highlighting key sentences containing keywords in order to support peer review. The selected sentences are supposed to help peer reviewers of articles in educational sciences to focus their attention on some relevant textual evidence for formulating their judgments. We have argued that even if the structural characteristics— the abstract, the keywords and the section headings—guide the reader in following the development of the article, content-oriented highlighting of key sentences might enhance the quick understanding of the core contents.

Although the subjects of educational science research articles display very heterogeneous structures and contents, the system could identify a number of sentences containing the main statements of the articles. Text-inherent developments not accompanied by structural signs like the outcomes of empirical studies or the contents of a theoretical discussion about abstract terms could be identified using automatic text analysis, which can possibly save intellectual effort of scientists. The time-consuming task of reviewing a growing number of research publications, hardly manageable when studying each submitted manuscript thoroughly, could thus be facilitated and supported and less threatened to be replaced by wholly automatic metric systems when time constraints become more severe.

The method we have developed is implemented in XIP, a rule-based dependency parser. It uses pre-existing lexical resources and applies the concept-matching framework.

The results of our first tests suggest that two of our three initial hypotheses are partially valid. According to our first hypothesis the key sentences relevant for peer reviewing are those that describe the problems, aims and results in the articles. We have found that sentences conveying definitions, especially in theoretical articles, should also be highlighted as key sentences. The second hypothesis is that these sentences can be detected using the concept-matching grammar. We have found in the majority of cases that this hypothesis is valid, however, enlarging the unit of concept-matching to multiple sentences would improve the performance.

Based on this result we are undertaking a user evaluation to measure the time needed to peer review these articles with and without highlighting. We are also planning to extend the system in the two directions suggested by the test results.

Besides providing assistance to peer reviewers the system presented here could be used in other applications, which we would like to explore in future projects. The possibilities include improving search functionalities in digital libraries, displaying electronic documents by linking keywords to key sentences and discourse-based navigation.

Acknowledgments

The research leading to these results has received funding from the European Community's Seventh Framework Programme under grant agreement n° 217549.

We would like to thank Alexander Botte, Aaron Kaplan, Peter Meyer and our partners in the EERQI project for their valuable contributions and suggestions.

References

Salah Aït-Mokhtar, Jean-Pierre Chanod, and Claude Roux. 2002. Robustness beyond shallowness: incremental dependency parsing. *Natural Language Engineering*, 8(2/3):121-144.

Robin Barrow. 2008. Education and the Body: Prolegomena. *British Journal of Educational Studies* 56(3):272-285.

Lutz Bornmann and Hans-Dieter Daniel. 2003. Begutachtung durch Fachkollegen in der Wissenschaft. Stand der Forschung zur Reliabilität, Fairness und Validität des Peer-Review-Verfahrens. *Universität auf dem Prüfstand. Konzepte und Befunde der Hochschulforschung. (S. Schwarz and U. Teichler, Eds.).* Campus Verlag Frankfurt/New York: 207-225.

Paul Brett. 1994. A genre analysis of the results section of sociology articles. *English for Specific Purposes*, 13(1):47-59.

David Bridges. 2008. Criteria of Quality in Educational Research. Working Group Report of the 1st EERQI Workshop, 20-21 June 2008. Leuven. Project Internal Document.

Javier Couto and Jean-Luc Minel. 2007. *NaviTexte : a Text Navigation Tool.* Artificial Intelligence and Human-Oriented Computing, Lecture Notes in Artificial Intelligence, 4733, Springer, Berlin, Heidelberg.

Susanne Fiedler. 1991. *Fachtextlinguistische Untersuchungen zum Kommunikationsbereich der Pädagogik dargestellt an relevanten Fachtextsorten im Englischen.* Lang, Frankfurt a.M.

Richard Holmes. 1997. Genre analysis, and the social sciences: An investigation of the structure of research article discussion sections in three disciplines. *English for Specific Purposes*, 16(4):321-337.

Noriko Kando. 1997. Text-level structure of research papers: Implications for text-based information processing systems. *Proceedings of the 19th British Computer Society Annual Colloquium of Information Retrieval Research*, Sheffield University, Sheffield, UK, 68-81.

Elizabeth D. Liddy. 1991. The discourse-level structure of empirical abstracts: an exploratory study. *Information Processing and Management*, 27(1):55-81.

Frédérique Lisacek, Christine Chichester, Aaron Kaplan, and Ágnes Sandor. 2005. Discovering paradigm shift patterns in biomedical abstracts: application to neurodegenerative diseases. *First International Symposium on Semantic Mining in Biomedicine*, Cambridge, UK, April 11-13, 2005.

Yanping Lu. 2005. Editorial Peer Review in Education: Mapping the Field. *Australian Association for Research in Education 2004 conference papers, Melbourne, Australia (Jeffery, P. L., Ed.):*1-19.

Yanping Lu. 2008. Peer review and its contribution to manuscript quality: an Australian perspective. *Learned Publishing*, 21(3):307-316.

Eric G. Meinberg and Peter J. Stern. 2003. Incidence of Wrong-Site Surgery Among Hand Surgeons. *The Journal of Bone and Joint Surgery (American)* 85:193-197.

Yoko Mizuta, Anna Korhonen, Tony Mullen, and Nigel Collier. 2006. Zone analysis in biology articles as a basis for information extraction. *International Journal of Medical Informatics*, 75(6):468-87.

Michaela Montesi and John Mackenzie Owen. 2008. Research journal articles as document genres: exploring their role in knowledge organization. *Journal of Documentation*, 64(1):143-167.

Robert N. Oddy, Elizabeth D. Liddy, Bhaskaran Balakrishnan, Ann Bishop, Joseph Elewononi and Eileen Martin. 1992. Towards the use of situational information in information retrieval. *Journal of Documentation*, 48(2):123-171.

Yang Ruiying and Desmond Allison. 2004. Research articles in applied linguistics: structures from a functional perspective. *English for Specific Purposes*, 23(3):264-279.

Ágnes Sándor, Aaron Kaplan and Gilbert Rondeau. 2006. Discourse and citation analysis with concept-matching. *International Symposium: Discourse and document (ISDD)*, Caen, France, June 15-16, 2006.

Ágnes Sándor. 2007. Modeling metadiscourse conveying the author's rhetorical strategy in biomedical research abstracts. *Revue Française de Linguistique Appliquée* 200(2):97-109.

Ágnes Sándor. 2009. Automatic detection of discourse indicating emerging risk. To appear in *Critical Approaches to Discourse Analysis across Disciplines. Risk as Discourse – Discourse as Risk: Interdisciplinary perspectives.*

Simone Teufel and Marc Moens. 2002. Summarizing scientific articles: experiments with relevance and rhetorical status. *Computational Linguistics*, 28(4):409-445.

Victoria Uren, Simon Buckingham Shum, Clara Mancini, and Gangmin Li. 2007. Modelling Naturalistic Argumentation in Research Literatures: Representation and Interaction Design Issues. *International Journal of Intelligent Systems, (Special Issue on Computational Models of Natural Argument, Eds: C. Reed and F. Grasso)*, 22(1):17-47.

Richard Whitley and Jochen Gläser. 2007. *The Changing Governance of Sciences: The Advent Of Research Evaluation Systems.* Springer

Designing a Citation-Sensitive Research Tool: An Initial Study of Browsing-Specific Information Needs

Stephen Wan†, **Cécile Paris**†, **Michael Muthukrishna**†, **Robert Dale**‡
† ICT Centre, CSIRO, Australia
Firstname.Lastname@csiro.au
‡Centre for Language Technology
Faculty of Science
Macquarie University, Australia
rdale@science.mq.edu.au

Abstract

Practitioners and researchers need to stay up-to-date with the latest advances in their fields, but the constant growth in the amount of literature available makes this task increasingly difficult. We investigated *the literature browsing task* via a user requirements analysis, and identified the information needs that biomedical researchers commonly encounter in this application scenario. Our analysis reveals that a number of literature-based research tasks are preformed which can be served by both generic and contextually tailored preview summaries. Based on this study, we describe the design of an implemented literature browsing support tool which helps readers of scientific literature decide whether or not to pursue and read a cited document. We present findings from a preliminary user evaluation, suggesting that our prototype helps users make relevance judgements about cited documents.

1 Introduction

Practitioners and researchers in all fields face a great challenge in attempting to keep up-to-date with the literature relevant to their work. In this context, search engines provide a useful tool for information discovery; but search is just one modality for gathering information. We also regularly read through documents and expect to find additional relevant information in referenced (cited or hyperlinked) documents. This results in a browsing-based activity, where we explore connections through related documents.

This browsing behaviour is increasingly supported today as publishers of scientific material deliver hyperlinked documents via a variety of media including Adobe's Portable Document Format (PDF) as well as the more conventional web hypertext format. Given appropriate document databases and knowledge of referencing conventions, it is relatively straightforward to support the automatic downloading of cited documents: such functionality already exists within reference managers such as *JabRef*[1] and *Sente*[2]. This 'blind downloading', however, does not address the question of the relevancy of the linked document for the reader at the time of reading. Apart from the publication details of the reference and the citation context, readers are provided with very little information on the basis of which to determine whether the cited document is worth exploring more thoroughly. Given the potentially large number of citations that may be encountered, this results in the following *browsing-specific scenario*: how can we help a user quickly determine whether the cited document is indeed worth downloading, perhaps paying for, and reading?

In the study presented here, we focussed on the needs of biomedical researchers, who are often time-poor and yet apparently spend 18% of their time gathering and reviewing information (Hersh, 2008). They regularly search through repositories of online scholarly literature to update their expert knowledge; in this domain, the penalty for not staying up-to-date with the latest advances can be severe, potentially affecting medical experiments. In our work, we found that two thirds of researchers regularly engaged in browsing scientific literature. Given the prevalent use of the browsing modality, we believe that novel research tools are needed to help readers make decisions about the relevance of cited material.

To better understand the user's information needs that arise when reading and browsing through academic literature, and to ascertain what NLP techniques we might be able to use to help support them, we conducted a user require-

[1] jabref.sourceforge.net
[2] www.thirdstreetsoftware.com

Proceedings of the 2009 Workshop on Text and Citation Analysis for Scholarly Digital Libraries, ACL-IJCNLP 2009, pages 45–53,
Suntec, Singapore, 7 August 2009.

ments analysis. It revealed a number of common problems faced by readers of scientific literature. These served to focus our efforts in designing and implementing a browsing support tool for scientific literature, referred to here as CSIBS.

CSIBS helps readers decide which cited documents to read by providing them with information which is useful at the point when citations are encountered. The application provides information about the cited document and identifies important sentences in that document, based on the user's current reading context. The key observation here is that the reading context can indicate *why* the reader might be interested in the cited document. In addition to meta-data about the cited document, and its abstract, a *contextualised preview* is shown within the same browser in which the citing document is being viewed (for example, Adobe Acrobat Reader or a web browser), thus avoiding an interruption to the user's primary reading activity. This contextualised preview contains important sentences from the cited document that are related to the reading context.

We present related work on understanding information needs in Section 2; we outline our user requirements analysis in the domain of scientific literature in Section 3; and the results of the analysis and our understanding of the browsing-specific information needs are presented in Section 4. In Section 5, we describe a tool developed to meet the most pressing of these information needs. Section 6 presents a feedback from an initial evaluation. We conclude by discussing our overall findings in Section 7.

2 Related Work

2.1 Information Needs

Existing work on information needs, beginning with Taylor (1962), typically focuses on mapping from a particular query to the underlying interest of the user. In a recent example of such work, Henrich and Luedecke (2007) describes methods for constructing lists of domain-specific key words which may correspond well to user interests. However, we are interested in relating information needs to user tasks in scenarios in which there is no explicit query, as in Bystrm et al. (1995); in particular, our work focuses on browsing scenarios. Toms (2000) presents a study of browsing behaviour over electronic texts and examines the differences between searching and browsing. In that work, browsing is performed across multiple news articles where the links between articles are inferred based on topic similarity. In contrast, we consider explicit hypertext links which are linguistically embedded in the document as citations, where the embedding text serves as link anchors.

2.2 Information Needs in Biomedicine

Ely et al. (2000) present an overview of the information needs of practicing clinicians, deriving a set of commonly asked questions. Although we are interested in doctors as users, the type of information needs presented in this paper relate to the activity of conducting scientific investigation, rather than that of treating a patient.

Task-based analyses of the biomedical domain have been studied by Bartlett and Neugebauer (2008) and Tran et al. (2004). Their analyses, like ours, are task-based and use qualitative studies to uncover the underlying uses of information. However, the tasks outlined in these related works are focused on a specific set of information needs in a research area: for example, the determination of a functional analysis of gene sequences. Our work differs in that we wish to take a more general view in order to elicit information needs to do with scientific research, at least at the level of biomedical sciences.

The information needs and tasks of academic users have been studied previously by Belkin (1994), who focuses on scholarly publications in the humanities domain. We perform an investigation along similar lines, but with a focus on academic literature used to conduct scientific research.

2.3 Using Scientific Literature

The genre of academic literature, and the development of technologies to support researchers as users, has been studied by several groups working in automatic text summarisation. Teufel and Moens (2002) describe a summarisation approach that extracts text from documents and highlights the rhetorical role that an extract plays within the originating document (for example, stating the *Aim* of an experiment). Qazvinian and Radev (2008) present an approach to summarising academic documents based on finding citation contexts in the entire set of published literature for the document in question. Both approaches, however, treat the cited document in isolation of the reading context and do not actively support the reading task.

3 Understanding How Researchers Browse through Scientific Literature

To determine what readers of scientific literature want to know about cited documents, we conducted a user requirements analysis. Our method is based on Grounded Theory (Glaser and Strauss, 1967), a commonly used approach in Human Computer Interaction (Corbin and Strauss, 2008). We began by interviewing subjects from an appropriate user demographic and recording their verbal descriptions about a real scenario situated in their day-to-day activities. Following this, we designed a questionnaire for wider participation which presented scenario-based questions attempting to uncover their information needs and tasks. Participants were asked to provide free text answers. The responses were then collated and analysed for commonalities, bringing to the fore those issues that were salient across the participants. We report on the questionnaire design and responses in this paper.

Beginning with such a study can reduce the risk of building tools that have only limited utility. This is particularly true of new and less understood application scenarios, such as the one explored here.

3.1 Questionnaire Design

An online questionnaire was used to reach participants who actively read academic literature.[3] To encourage participation, the questionnaire was limited to 10 questions, which were formulated independently of any particular scientific domain.

We were explicit about the aims of the questionnaire by providing an initial brief, stating that the feedback from participants would be used to develop new tools for browsing through scientific literature. Within the questionnaire, to prepare participants for our scenario-based questions, the first few questions were basic and concerned the general usage of scientific literature. For example, we asked about the high-level reasons for which they used scientific literature (e.g., 'To learn about a new topic'; 'To update your knowledge on a particular topic'). Participants could also specify their own reasons. In addition, we also asked them about the frequency of their literature browsing activity.

The main section of the questionnaire consisted of a series of questions, corresponding to the issues we wanted to explore:

1. What information needs do researchers have of a cited document, and what specific tasks does this information serve?
2. What makes it difficult for researchers to find the answers to their questions about cited documents?
3. What tasks are potential targets for automation?

Questions were to be answered with free text responses, focussed by presenting a scenario in which the researcher encounters a citation whilst reading a scientific publication. The first question above aims to better understand the researchers' information needs and tasks; the second and third are concerned with ideas for potential applications which could benefit from NLP and IR research.

To address the first research issue, participants were asked to recall a recent experience in which, while reading a publication, they had encountered a citation. Within this context, participants were asked to describe what questions they may have had of the cited document. To clarify how these questions relate to a specific context of use, respondents were then asked to relate the questions they identified back to some task undertaken as part of their research work.

Responses regarding the difficulties encountered in satisfying information needs were collected with respect to the participants earlier responses. So as to not bias the participant, the question was phrased neutrally. We asked what aspects of scientific literature and current technology made it easy or hard to find answers to the participants' personal research questions. We examined responses with the aim of determining how technology might reduce the burden of knowledge discovery. Responses were again focused by using the same scenario as in the previous question.

The third research issue was explored via two separate questions. The first presented the participants with a scenario in which they had access to a non-expert human assistant who could perform one or more simple tasks identified in their earlier responses; they were then asked what kinds

[3]The online questionnaire tool, SurveyMonkey (www.surveymonkey.com), was used to implement the questionnaire as an online interactive form.

of tasks they would delegate to such an assistant. A second, more direct, question was presented requiring participants to describe which tools they would like to use, or to suggest new tools that would help them in the future, when it came to browsing through scientific literature.

Finally, optional questions about the participants' research backgrounds were presented at the end of the questionnaire. These were deliberately placed last to reduce barriers to completion.

4 Questionnaire Data Analysis

4.1 Analysing the Results

We recruited users with a background in biomedical life sciences since we had access to an extensive corpus of documents in this domain with which to build some kind of application. Note, however, that our questions were not specific to this domain, and the questionnaire could potentially be re-run with participants from a different scientific background.

We contacted 36 users who might be interested in life sciences publications. Of these, 24 participants started the questionnaire, and 18 completed it. Of the 24 participants, two thirds indicated that they browsed through academic literature at least once a week.

The written responses were separately analysed by three of the authors. Responses to each question were examined, checking for repeated terms and concepts that could form the basis of clustering. Salient information needs were matched to corresponding tasks, and commonly mentioned areas of difficulty and suggestions for delegation were grouped. Once each author had performed his or her own analysis, the salient groupings for each question were collaboratively determined, consolidating the three analyses performed in isolation. The most salient groupings were then examined for potential tasks that might be automated.

4.2 Questionnaire Data

We now present the results of the analysis. These are organised with respect to each of the three research issues.

4.2.1 Questions of the Cited Document

Figure 1 presents the most frequently indicated information needs and the most frequent tasks that were identified. The information needs can be grouped into two main categories. The first, which we refer to as *meta-data needs*, refers to information about the document external to the document content itself. These needs could be met by a series of database queries *about* the document, involving, for example, the author information and the citation counts for the document. We note that, often, the abstract can also be retrieved via a database query (and thus does not require any in-depth text analysis of the cited document), although technically this is not meta-data. In terms of the underlying task, this kind of generic information may be used in *deciding whether to trust the cited source.*

Information Needs	Freq
[md] About accessing the full text	9
[co] Article details (Definition, Methods, Results)	7
[md] About the authors	6
[md] About the publication date	5
[co] About relevance to own work	4
[md] The abstract	3
[co] The references	3

Participant Task	Freq
Deciding whether to believe the citation	4
Finding baselines for experiments	3
Comparing own ideas to article	3
Finding information to justify the citation	3
Finding information about methods	2
Finding additional references	2
Updating clinical knowledge	2
Conducting a survey of the literature	2
Identifying key researchers in the field	2
Updating research knowledge	2

Figure 1: Principal information needs and tasks of participants with regard to citations. In the first table, information needs are prefixed by 'md' for *meta-data* and 'co' for *content-oriented*. 'Freq' indicates the number of occurrences in the results.

The second category of information needs, which we refer to as being *content-oriented*, can be met by providing information sourced from *within* the cited document. This type of information facilitates multiple tasks. For example, these might include understanding why a document was cited, or finding new baselines to design new experiments. We refer to these tasks in general as *citation-focused*, as some underlying information need is triggered by the text that the participant has just read, whether this is for advancing one's understanding of a topic, or pursuing a specific line of scientific inquiry.

4.2.2 Difficulties in Finding Answers

This question required participants to voluntarily reflect on their own research practices, a process that is influenced partially by their expertise in research and their exposure to different research tools. Some responses described features of software that were appealing, while others related to the difficulties faced by researchers in finding relevant information. In this paper, we present only the subset of responses that concern the difficulties encountered, since this will influence the functionality of new research tools. These responses are presented in Figure 2.

Difficulties	Freq
Finding the exact text to justify the citation	3
Poor writing	2
Comparing documents	1
Resolving references to the same object	1

Figure 2: Difficulties in finding information.

In general, the difficulties concerned some kind of analysis of text. We note that these tasks are largely citation-focused, requiring content-oriented information. Examples of comments regarding this task are presented in Figure 3. For example, participants wanted to know how the cited document compared the citing document from the perspective of experimental design. However, the citation-focused task that was most commonly mentioned as difficult was that of justifying citations. Participants mentioned that reading through the entire cited document for this purpose was a tedious task, particularly when looking for information in poorly written documents.

Citation usually does not include the position of the information in the cited article . . . it might be necessary to read all of the article to find it in another reference and so on.

If the first report was only citing the second report for a small piece of information, that *information may be hard to locate* in the second report.

The original reference may have just cited a very small component of the second report, either just a comment made in the discussion or a supplemental figure . . . *It may take a while to locate and justify the citation* if it isn't the major finding of the report.

If I see a citation in a report that I am interested in, *I generally want to know if the cited report actually supports the statement in the original report.* Very often – way too often – citations do not. For all important citations I track down the original cited work and verify that it actually says what it is supposed to.

Figure 3: Some sample responses from users with regard to justifying citations; emphases added.

4.2.3 Tasks for Automation

Our analysis of responses to the task automation questions revealed two interesting outcomes: delegation occurred often with the use of key words, and participants expressed the need for tools to express relationships between domain concepts. These are presented in Figure 4.

Automation Possibilities	Freq
Search cited document for key words	4
Search for further publications using key words	3
Refine search using related concepts	6

Figure 4: Potential candidates for a new research tool.

Responses to the question regarding task delegation revealed that for research-oriented tasks, participants felt the need to direct assistants through the use of key words. This is consistent to responses to earlier questions detailing what aspects of current technology were attractive, including user interface conventions such as key word highlighting. Otherwise, the other reported delegated task was that of simple database entry of publication records. We interpret these responses as indicating that participants are not overly willing to hand over responsibility for complex tasks to assistants. If delegation of more research-oriented activities occurs, participants want to understand how and why results were obtained. While responses were made assuming delegation to human assistants, we believe that such issues are even more crucial for results obtained via automated means.

Suggested novel features centered upon a better representation of relationships between domain concepts to be used for query refinement. Responses included expressions such as "refined search", a handling of user-specified "mind maps" (for repeated searches), and the use of "trails" explaining how results connected to search terms, key words and the author.

5 Prototype Requirements

As a result of these findings, we chose to build a tool that meets the two types of information needs revealed in the initial user requirements study. The purpose of the resulting tool, CSIBS, is to help readers prioritise which cited documents are worth spending time to download and read further. In this way, CSIBS helps readers to browse and navigate through a dense network of cited documents.

To facilitate this task in accordance with the elicited user requirements, CSIBS produces an alternate version of a published article that has been prepared with pop-up previews of cited documents. Each preview contains meta-data, the abstract and content-oriented information. It is provided to the user to help perform research tasks that arise as a consequence of encountering a citation and needing to investigate further. The preview is not intended to serve as a surrogate for the cited document. Rather, it is aimed at helping readers make relevance judgements about citations.

The meta-data helps the user to appraise the citation and to make a value judgement about the work cited. The abstract provides a generic summary of the cited document, indicating the scope of the work cited. The content-oriented information supports any *citation-focused* tasks, for example citation justification, through the provision of detailed information sourced from within the cited document. We refer to this as a *Contextualised Preview*. It is constructed using automatic text summarisation techniques that tailor the resulting summary to the user's current interests, here approximately represented by the citation context: that is, the sentence in which the citation is linguistically embedded. We briefly describe CSIBS, in this section; for a full description, see Wan et al. (2009).

Each preview appears in a pop-up text box activated by moving the mouse over the citation. The specific interaction (a double click versus a "mouse-over") depends on whether the article is displayed via a web browser or as a PDF document. Figure 5 shows the resulting pop-up for the PDF display.

5.1 A Meta-Data Summary and Abstract

Participants often wanted a generic summary outlining the overall scope and contributions of the cited work. This is typically available via the abstract. Additionally, CSIBS presents a variety of meta-data returned from queries to an online publications database:[4]

- The full reference: This provides readers with the date of publication and the journal title, amongst other things.
- Author Information: CSIBS can include data to help the reader establish a level of trust in the citation, primarily focusing on information about the authors' affiliations and the number of related citations in the research area.
- The citation count for the cited document: Participants indicated that this was useful in appraising the cited article.

These pieces of information were commonly identified as useful in helping readers make value judgements about the cited work. This is perhaps an artifact of the biomedical domain, where research has a critical nature and concerns health and medical issues.

5.2 A Contextualised Preview

To generate the contextualised preview of the cited document, the system finds the set of sentences that relate to the citation context, employing approaches for summarising documents that exploit anchor text (Wan and Paris, 2008). Following Spark Jones (1998), we specify the *purpose* of the contextualised summary along particular dimensions, indicated here in italics:

- The *situation* is tied to a particular context of use: an in-browser summary triggered by a citation and its citing context.
- An *audience* of expert researchers is assumed.
- The intended *usage* of the summary is one of preview. We assume that the reader is making a relevance judgement as to whether or not to download (and, if necessary, buy) the cited document. Specifically, the information presented should help the reader determine the level of trust to place in the document, understand why the article is cited, and decide whether or not to read it.
- The summary is intended only to provide a partial *coverage* of the whole document, specifically focused on content that directly relates to the citation context.
- The style of the summary is intended to be *indicative*. That is, it should present specific

[4] `www.embase.com`

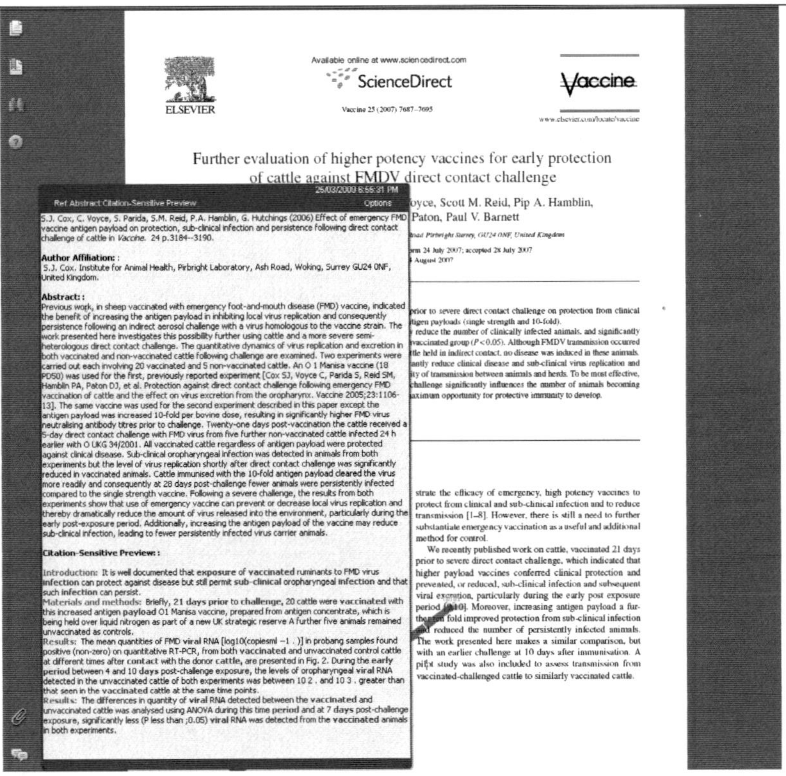

Figure 5: A sample pop-up with an automatically generated summary, triggered by a mouse action over the citation. Extracted sentences are grouped together by section titles. Words that match with the citation context are coloured and emboldened.

details to facilitate a relevance judgement, allowing the user to determine if the cited document can be used to source more information on a topic, as opposed to just mentioning it in passing.

To create the preview summary, the cited document is downloaded from a publisher's database[5] in its XML form and then segmented into sections, paragraphs and sentences. Each sentence in the cited document is compared with the citation context in order to find the best justification sentences for that particular citation. Due to the limited space available in the pop-up, the number of extracted sentences is capped at a predefined limit, currently set to four. Using vector space methods (Salton and McGill, 1983) weighted with term frequency (and omitting stop words), the best matching sentence is defined as the one scoring the highest on the cosine similarity metric with the citation context. The attractiveness of this approach lies in its simplicity, resulting in a fast computation of a preview (≈ 0.03 seconds), making the process amenable to batch processing of multiple documents or, in the future, live generation of previews at runtime. To help with the readability of the resulting preview, the system also extracts structural information from the cited document. In particular, for each extracted sentence, the system identifies the section in which it belongs; the extracted sentences are then grouped by section, and presented with their section headings, as illustrated in Figure 5.

CSIBS focuses on returning precise results, so that the system does not exacerbate any existing information overload problems by burdening the reader with poorly matching sentences. To achieve this, we currently use exact matches to words in the citation context; in on-going work, we are exploring methods to relax this constraint without hurting performance. In line with our user requirements analysis, we have designed the tool so that the user is able to easily see how the summary was constructed. Matching tokens are highlighted, allowing the reader to understand why specific sen-

[5] `www.sciencedirect.com`

tences were extracted.

6 Initial Feedback

6.1 Evaluation Overview

We built a prototype version of CSIBS and conducted a preliminary qualitative evaluation. The goal was to examine how participants would react to the pop-up previews. The feedback allows us to further clarify our analysis and subsequent development.

We asked participants to view a number of pop-up previews in order to answer the question: *Is the Citation Justified?* This was one of the more difficult questions that researchers found challenging when making a relevancy judgement. The actual judgements are not important in this evaluation. Instead, we gauged the reported utility of the prototype based on the participants' self-reported confidence when performing the task. To capture this information, participants were asked to score their confidence on a 3-point Likert scale.

Three biomedical researchers, all of whom had taken part in our original user requirements analysis, participated in the evaluation. Each participant was shown nine different passages containing a citation context, each situated in a different *FEBS Letters*[6] publication (which was also presented in full to the participants). At each viewing of a citation context, two supporting texts were provided with which the participant was asked to answer the citation justification question. For all participants, the first supporting text was produced by a baseline system that simply provided the full reference of the citation. The second was either the abstract or the contextualised preview, which in this evaluation was limited to three sentences. Meta-data was not presented for this study as we specifically wanted feedback on the citation justification task.

The small sample size does not permit hypothesis testing. However, we are encouraged by the comparable positive gains in self-reported confidence scores (Abstract: +1.2 versus CSIBS: +2.2) compared to simply showing the full reference. Since both preview types were positive, we assume that these types of information facilitated the relevance judgements. Participants also reported that, for the contextualised preview, 2 out of 3 sentences were found to be useful on average.

[6]The journal of the Federation of Europeans Biochemical Societies.

The qualitative feedback also supported CSIBS. One participant made some particularly interesting observations regarding selected sentences and the structure of the cited document. Specifically, useful sentences tended to be located deeper in the cited document, for example in the methods sections This participant suggested that, for an expert user, showing sentences from the earlier sections of a publication was not useful; for the same reason, the abstract might be too general and not helpful in justifying a citation. Finally, this participant remarked that, in those situations where each document downloaded from a proprietary repository incurs a fee, the citation-sensitive previews would be very useful in deciding whether to download the document.

7 Conclusions

In this paper, we presented an analysis of browsing-specific information needs in the domain of scientific literature. In this context, users have information needs that are not realised as search queries; rather these remain implicit in the minds of users as they browse through hyperlinked documents. Our analysis sheds light on these information needs, and the tasks being performed in their pursuit, using a set of scenario-based questions.

The analysis revealed two tasks often performed by participants: the appraisal task and the citation-focused task. CSIBS was designed to support the underlying needs by providing meta-data information, the abstract, and a contextualised preview for each citation. The user requirement of search refinement was not directly addressed in this work, but could be met by techniques of query refinement in IR, synonym-based expansion in summarisation, and of course, additional user specified key terms. In future work, we will explore these possibilities. Our results to date are encouraging for the use of NLP techniques to support readers prioritise which cited documents to read when browsing through scientific literature.

Acknowledgments

We would like to thank all the participants who took part in our study. We would also like to thank Julien Blondeau and Ilya Anisimoff, who helped to implement the prototype.

References

Joan C. Bartlett and Tomasz Neugebauer. 2008. A task-based information retrieval interface to support bioinformatics analysis. In *IIiX '08: Proceedings of the second international symposium on Information interaction in context*, pages 97–101, New York, NY, USA. ACM.

Nicholas J. Belkin. 1994. Design principles for electronic textual resources: Investigating users and uses of scholarly information. In *Current Issues in Computational Linguistics: In Honour of Donald Walker.Kluwer*, pages 1–18. Kluwer.

Katriina Bystrm, Katriina Murtonen, Kalervo Jrvelin, Kalervo Jrvelin, and Kalervo Jrvelin. 1995. Task complexity affects information seeking and use. In *Information Processing and Management*, pages 191–213.

Juliet Corbin and Anselm L. Strauss. 2008. *Basics of qualitative research : techniques and procedures for developing grounded theory*. Sage, 3rd edition.

John W Ely, Jerome A Osheroff, Paul N Gorman, Mark H Ebell, M Lee Chambliss, Eric A Pifer, and P Zoe Stavri. 2000. A taxonomy of generic clinical questions: classification study. *British Medical Journal*, 321:429–432.

Barney G. Glaser and Anselm L. Strauss. 1967. *The Discovery of Grounded Theory: Strategies for Qualitative Research*. Aldine de Gruyter, New York.

Andreas Henrich and Volker Luedecke. 2007. Characteristics of geographic information needs. In *GIR '07: Proceedings of the 4th ACM workshop on Geographical information retrieval*, pages 1–6, New York, NY, USA. ACM.

W. R. Hersh. 2008. *Information Retrieval*. Springer. Information Retrieval for biomedical researchers.

Vahed Qazvinian and Dragomir R. Radev. 2008. Scientific paper summarization using citation summary networks. In *The 22nd International Conference on Computational Linguistics (COLING 2008)*, Machester, UK, August.

G. Salton and M. J. McGill. 1983. *Introduction to modern information retrieval*. McGraw-Hill, New York.

Karen Spark Jones. 1998. Automatic summarizing: factors and directions. In I. Mani and M. Maybury, editors, *Advances in Automatic Text Summarisation*. MIT Press, Cambridge MA.

Robert S Taylor. 1962. Process of asking questions. *American Documentation*, 13:391–396, October.

Simone Teufel and Marc Moens. 2002. Summarizing scientific articles: experiments with relevance and rhetorical status. *Computional Linguistics*, 28(4):409–445.

Elaine G. Toms. 2000. Understanding and facilitating the browsing of electronic text. *International Journal of Human-Computing Studies*, 52(3):423–452.

D Tran, C Dubay, P Gorman, and W. Hersh. 2004. Applying task analysis to describe and facilitate bioinformatics tasks. *Studies in Health Technology and Informatics*, 107107(Pt 2):818–22.

Stephen Wan and Cécile Paris. 2008. In-browser summarisation: Generating elaborative summaries biased towards the reading context. In *The 46th Annual Meeting of the Association for Computational Linguistics: Human Language Technologies: Short Paper*, Columbus, Ohio, June.

Stephen Wan, Cécile Paris, and Robert Dale. 2009. Whetting the appetite of scientists: Producing summaries tailored to the citation context. In *Proceedings of the Joint Conference on Digital Libraries*.

The ACL Anthology Network Corpus

Dragomir R. Radev[1,2], Pradeep Muthukrishnan[1], Vahed Qazvinian[1]
[1]Department of Electrical Engineering and Computer Science
[2]School of Information
University of Michigan
{radev,mpradeep,vahed}@umich.edu

Abstract

We introduce the ACL Anthology Network (AAN), a manually curated networked database of citations, collaborations, and summaries in the field of Computational Linguistics. We also present a number of statistics about the network including the most cited authors, the most central collaborators, as well as network statistics about the paper citation, author citation, and author collaboration networks.

1 Introduction

The ACL Anthology is one of the most successful initiatives of the ACL. It was initiated by Steven Bird and is now maintained by Min Yen Kan. It includes all papers published by ACL and related organizations as well as the Computational Linguistics journal over a period of four decades. It is available at http://www.aclweb.org/anthology-new/ .

One fundamental problem with the ACL Anthology, however, is the fact that it is just a collection of papers. It doesn't include any citation information or any statistics about the productivity of the various researchers who contributed papers to it. We embarked on an ambitious initiative to manually annotate the entire Anthology in order to make it possible to compute such statistics.

In addition, we were able to use the annotated data for extracting citation summaries of all papers in the collection and we also annotated each paper by the gender of the authors (and are currently in the process of doing similarly for their institutions) in the goal of creating multiple gold standard data sets for training automated systems for performing such tasks.

2 Curation

The ACL Anthology includes 13,739 papers (excluding book reviews and posters). Each of the papers was converted from pdf to text using an OCR tool (www.pdfbox.org). After this conversion, we extracted the references semi-automatically using string matching. The above process outputs all the references as a single block so we then manually inserted line breaks between references. These references were then manually matched to other papers in the ACL Anthology using a "k-best" (with k = 5) string matching algorithm built into a CGI interface. A snapshot of this interface is shown in Figure 1. The matched references were stored together to produce the citation network. References to publications outside of the AAN were recorded but not included in the network.

In order to fix the issue of wrong author names and multiple author identities we had to perform a lot of manual post-processing. The first names and the last names were swapped for a lot of authors. For example, the author name "Caroline Brun" was present as "Brun Caroline" in some of her papers. Another big source of error was the exclusion of middle names or initials in a number of papers. For example, Julia Hirschberg had two identities as "Julia Hirschberg" and "Julia B. Hirschberg". There were a few spelling mistakes, like "Madeleine Bates" was misspelled as "Medeleine Bates".

Finally, many papers included incorrect titles in their citation sections. Some used the wrong years and/or venues as well.

Proceedings of the 2009 Workshop on Text and Citation Analysis for Scholarly Digital Libraries, ACL-IJCNLP 2009, pages 54–61,
Suntec, Singapore, 7 August 2009.

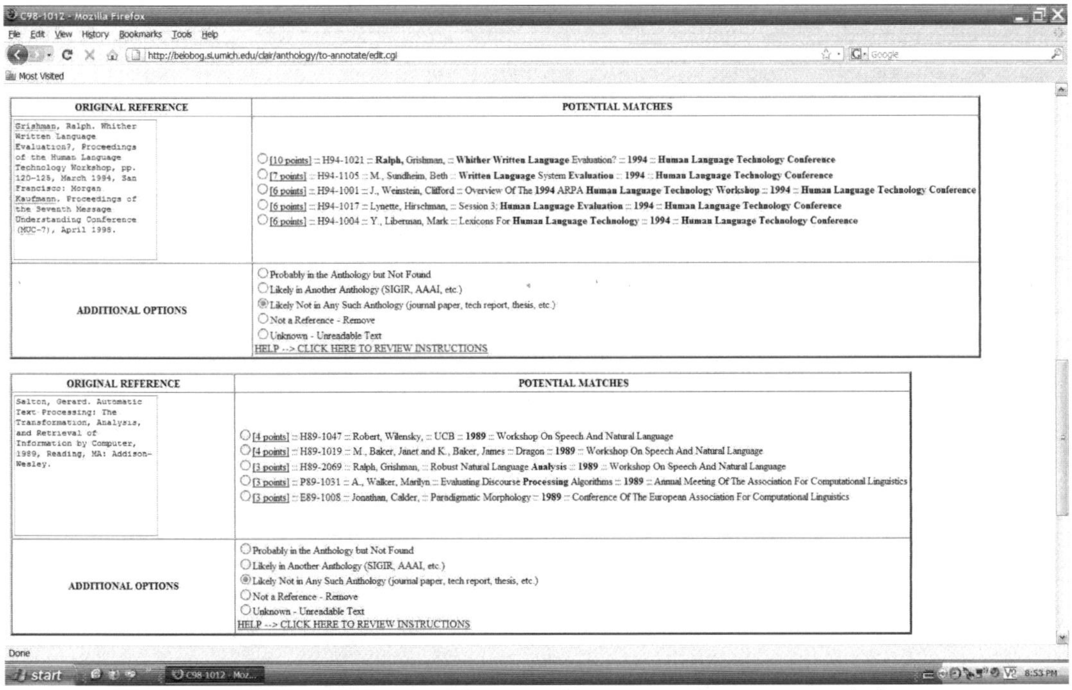

Figure 1: CGI interface used for matching new references to existing papers

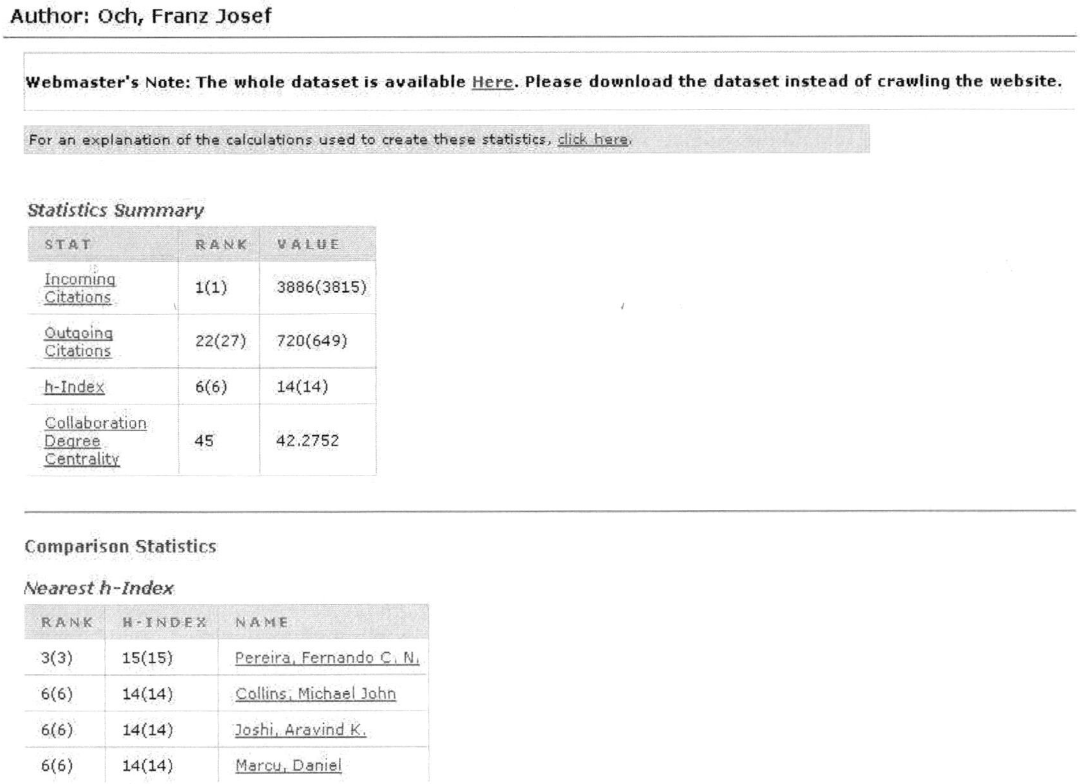

Figure 2: Snapshot of the different statistics computed for an author

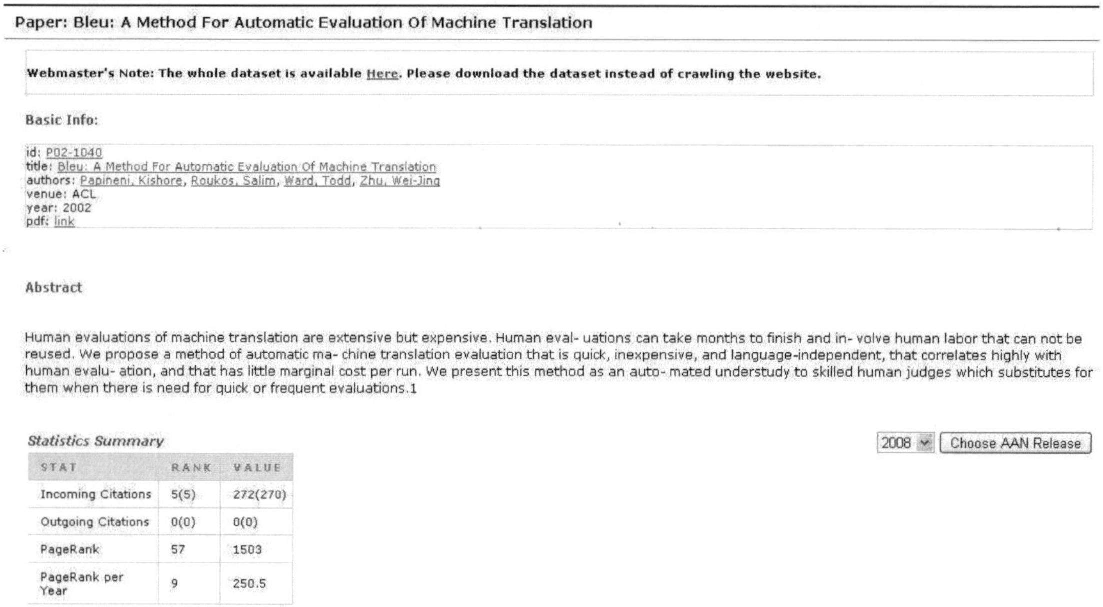

Figure 3: Snapshot of the different statistics for a paper

3 Statistics

Using the metadata and the citations extracted after curation, we have built three different networks.

The paper citation network is a directed network with each node representing a paper labeled with an ACL ID number and the edges representing a citation within that paper to another paper represented by an ACL ID. The paper citation network consists of 13,739 papers and 54,538 citations.

The author citation network and the author collaboration network are additional networks derived from the paper citation network. In both of these networks a node is created for each unique author. In the author citation network an edge is an occurrence of an author citing another author. For example, if a paper written by Franz Josef Och cites a paper written by Joshua Goodman, then an edge is created between Franz Josef Och and Joshua Goodman. Self citations cause self loops in the author citation network. The author citation network consists of 11,180 unique authors and 332,815 edges (196,905 edges if duplicates are removed).

In the author collaboration network, an edge is created for each collaboration. For example, if a paper is written by Franz Josef Och and Hermann Ney, then an edge is created between the two authors.

Table 1 shows some brief statistics about the first two releases of the data set (2006 and 2007). Table 2 describes the most current release of the data set (from 2008).

	2006		
	Paper citation network	Author citation network	Author collaboration network
n	8898	7849	7849
m	8765	137,007	41,362
	2007		
	Paper citation network	Author citation network	Author collaboration network
n	9767	9421	9421
m	44,142	158,479	45,878

Table 1: Growth of citation volume

	Paper Citation Network	**Author Citation Network**	**Author Collaboration Network**
Nodes	13,739	10,409	10,409
Edges	54,538	195,505	57,614
Diameter	22	10	20
Average	9.34	43.11	11.07

Degree			
Largest Connected Component	11,409	9061	7910
Watts Strogatz clustering coefficient	0.18	0.46	0.65
Newman clustering coefficient	0.07	0.14	0.36
clairlib avg. directed shortest path	5.91	3.32	5.87
Ferrer avg. directed shortest path	5.35	3.29	4.66
harmonic mean geodesic distance	63.93	5.47	9.40
harmonic mean geodesic distance with self-loops counted	63.94	5.47	9.40

Table 2: Network Statistics of the citation and collaboration network. The remaining authors (11,180-10,409) are not cited and are therefore removed from the network analysis

	Paper Citation Network	Author Citation Network	Author Collaboration Network
In-degree Stats			
Power Law Exponent	2.50	2.20	3.17
Power Law Relationship?	No	No	No
Newman Power Law exponent	2.00	1.55	2.18
Out-degree stats			
Power Law Exponent	3.70	2.56	3.17
Power Law Relationship?	No	No	No
Newman Power Law exponent	2.12	1.54	2.18
Total Degree Stats			
Power Law Exponent	2.72	2.27	3.17
Power Law Relationship?	No	No	No
Newman Power Law exponent	1.81	1.46	2.18

Table 3: Degree Statistics of the citation and collaboration networks

A lot of different statistics have been computed based on the data set release in 2007 by Radev et al. The statistics include PageRank scores which eliminate PageRank's inherent bias towards older papers, Impact factor, correlations between different measures of impact like H-Index, total number of incoming citations, PageRank. They also report results from a regression analysis using H-Index scores from different sources (AAN, Google Scholar) in an attempt to identify multi-disciplinary authors.

4 Sample rankings

This section shows some of the rankings that were computed using AAN.

Rank	*Icit*	*Title*
1	590	Building A Large Annotated Corpus Of English: The Penn Treebank
2	444	The Mathematics Of Statistical Machine Translation: Parameter Estimation
3	324	Attention Intentions And The Structure Of Discourse
4	271	A Maximum Entropy Approach To Natural Language Processing
5	270	Bleu: A Method For Automatic Evaluation Of
6	246	A Maximum-Entropy-Inspired Parser
7	230	A Stochastic Parts Program And Noun Phrase Parser For Unrestricted Text
8	221	A Systematic Comparison Of Various Statistical Alignment
9	211	A Maximum Entropy Model For Part-Of-Speech Tagging
10	211	Three Generative Lexicalized Models For Statistical Parsing

Table 4: Papers with the most incoming citations (icit)

Rank	*PR*	*Title*
1	1099.1	A Stochastic Parts Program And Noun Phrase Parser For Unrestricted Text
2	943.8	Finding Clauses In Unrestricted Text By Finitary And Stochastic Methods
3	568.8	A Stochastic Approach To
4	543.1	A Statistical Approach To Machine Translation
5	414.1	Building A Large Annotated Corpus Of English: The Penn Treebank
6	364.9	The Mathematics Of Statistical Machine Translation: Parameter Estimation
7	362.2	The Contribution Of Parsing To Prosodic Phrasing In An Experimental Text-To-Speech System
8	301.6	Attention Intentions And The Structure Of Discourse
9	250.5	Bleu: A Method For Automatic Evaluation Of Machine Translation
10	242.5	A Maximum Entropy Approach To Natural Language

Table 5: Papers with highest PageRank (PR) scores

It must be noted that the PageRank scores are not accurate because of the lack of citations outside AAN. Specifically, out of the 155,858 total number of citations, only 54,538 are within AAN.

Rank	*Icit*	*Author Name*
1 (1)	3886 (3815)	Och, Franz Josef
2 (2)	3297 (3119)	Ney, Hermann
3 (3)	3067 (3049)	Della Pietra, Vincent J.
4 (5)	2746 (2720)	Mercer, Robert L.
5 (4)	2741 (2724)	Della Pietra, Stephen
6 (6)	2605 (2589)	Marcus, Mitchell P.
7 (8)	2454 (2407)	Collins, Michael John
8 (7)	2451 (2433)	Brown, Peter F.
9 (9)	2428 (2390)	Church, Kenneth Ward
10 (10)	2047 (1991)	Marcu, Daniel

Table 6: Authors with most incoming citations (the values in parentheses are using non-self- citations)

Rank	*h*	*Author Name*
1	18	Knight, Kevin
2	16	Church, Kenneth Ward
3	15	Manning, Christopher D.
3	15	Grishman, Ralph
3	15	Pereira, Fernando C. N.
6	14	Marcu, Daniel
6	14	Och, Franz Josef
6	14	Ney, Hermann
6	14	Joshi, Aravind K.
6	14	Collins, Michael John

Table 7: Authors with the highest h-index

Rank	*ASP*	*Author Name*
1	2.977	Hovy, Eduard H.
2	2.989	Palmer, Martha Stone
3	3.011	Rambow, Owen
4	3.033	Marcus, Mitchell P.
5	3.041	Levin, Lori S.
6	3.052	Isahara. Hitoshi
7	3.055	Flickinger, Daniel P.
8	3.071	Klavans, Judith L.
9	3.073	Radev, Dragomir R.
10	3.077	Grishman, Ralph

Table 8: Authors with the least average shortest path (ASP) length in the author collaboration network

5 Related phrases

We have also computed the related phrases for every author using the text from the papers they have authored, using the simple TF-IDF scoring scheme (see Figure 4).

Closest Words/Phrase

	WORD	TF-IDF
1	alignment	3060.28788645363
2	translation	1609.64150036477
3	bleu	1270.66151594014
4	rouge	1131.61343683879
5	och	1070.2577306796
6	ney	1032.93379864255
7	alignments	938.646118573016
8	translations	779.35942419005
9	prime	606.568302266622
10	training	562.098194260184

Figure 4: Snapshot of the related phrases for Franz Josef Och

6 Citation summaries

The citation summary of an article, *P*, is the set of sentences that appear in the literature and cite *P*. These sentences usually mention at least one of the cited paper's contributions. We use AAN to extract the citation summaries of all articles, and thus the citation summary of *P* is a self-contained set and only includes the citing sentences that appear in AAN papers. Extraction is performed automatically using string-based heuristics by matching the citation pattern, author names and publication year, within the sentences. The following example shows the citation summary extracted for "Koo, Terry, Carreras, Xavier, Collins, Michael John, Simple Semi-supervised Dependency Parsing". The citation summary of (Koo et al., 2008) mentions KCC08, dependency parsing, and the use of word clustering in semi-supervised NLP.

C08-1051 1 7:191 Furthermore, recent studies revealed that word clustering is useful for semi-supervised learning in NLP (Miller et al., 2004; Li and McCallum, 2005; Kazama and Torisawa, 2008; Koo et al., 2008).

D08-1042 2 78:214 There has been a lot of progress in learning dependency tree parsers (McDonald et al., 2005; Koo et al., 2008; Wang et al., 2008).

W08-2102 3 194:209 The method shows improvements over the method described in (Koo et al., 2008), which is a state-of-the-art second-order dependency parser similar to that of (McDonald and Pereira, 2006), suggesting that the incorporation of constituent structure can improve dependency accuracy.

W08-2102 4 32:209 The model also recovers dependencies with significantly higher accuracy than state-of-the-art dependency parsers such as (Koo et al., 2008; McDonald and Pereira, 2006).

W08-2102 5 163:209 KCC08 unlabeled is from (Koo et al., 2008), a model that has previously been shown to have higher accuracy than (McDonald and Pereira, 2006).

W08-2102 6 164:209 KCC08 labeled is the labeled dependency parser from (Koo et al., 2008); here we only evaluate the unlabeled accuracy.

Figure 5: Sample citation summary

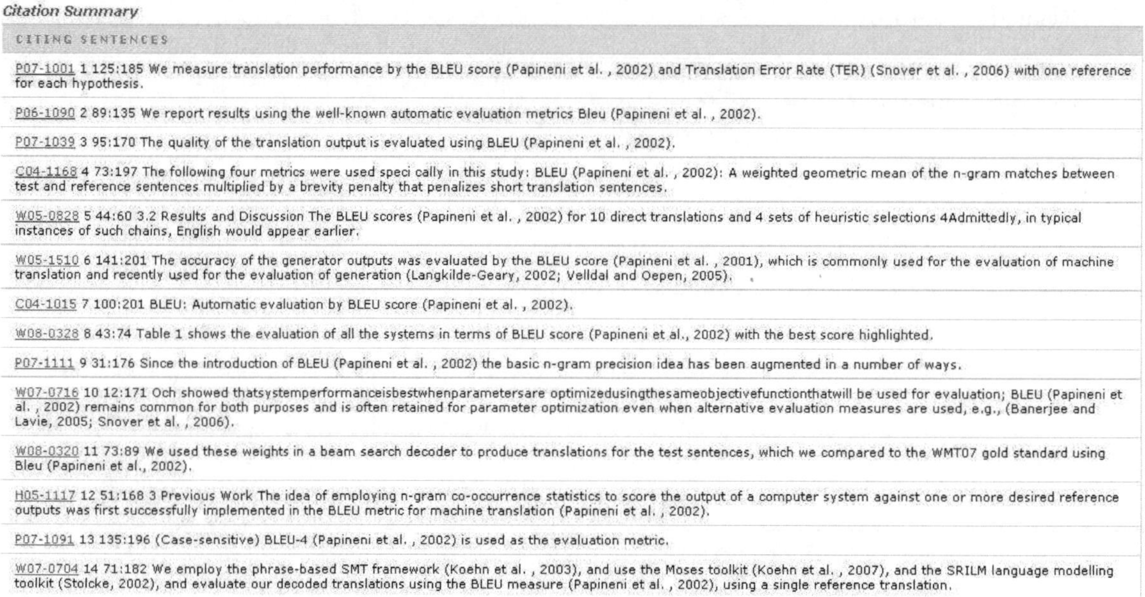

Citation Summary

CITING SENTENCES

P07-1001 1 125:185 We measure translation performance by the BLEU score (Papineni et al. , 2002) and Translation Error Rate (TER) (Snover et al. , 2006) with one reference for each hypothesis.

P06-1090 2 89:135 We report results using the well-known automatic evaluation metrics Bleu (Papineni et al. , 2002).

P07-1039 3 95:170 The quality of the translation output is evaluated using BLEU (Papineni et al. , 2002).

C04-1168 4 73:197 The following four metrics were used speci cally in this study: BLEU (Papineni et al. , 2002): A weighted geometric mean of the n-gram matches between test and reference sentences multiplied by a brevity penalty that penalizes short translation sentences.

W05-0828 5 44:60 3.2 Results and Discussion The BLEU scores (Papineni et al. , 2002) for 10 direct translations and 4 sets of heuristic selections 4Admittedly, in typical instances of such chains, English would appear earlier.

W05-1510 6 141:201 The accuracy of the generator outputs was evaluated by the BLEU score (Papineni et al. , 2001), which is commonly used for the evaluation of machine translation and recently used for the evaluation of generation (Langkilde-Geary, 2002; Velldal and Oepen, 2005).

C04-1015 7 100:201 BLEU: Automatic evaluation by BLEU score (Papineni et al. , 2002).

W08-0328 8 43:74 Table 1 shows the evaluation of all the systems in terms of BLEU score (Papineni et al., 2002) with the best score highlighted.

P07-1111 9 31:176 Since the introduction of BLEU (Papineni et al. , 2002) the basic n-gram precision idea has been augmented in a number of ways.

W07-0716 10 12:171 Och showed thatsystemperformanceisbestwhenparametersare optimizedusingthesameobjectivefunctionthatwill be used for evaluation; BLEU (Papineni et al. , 2002) remains common for both purposes and is often retained for parameter optimization even when alternative evaluation measures are used, e.g., (Banerjee and Lavie, 2005; Snover et al. , 2006).

W08-0320 11 73:89 We used these weights in a beam search decoder to produce translations for the test sentences, which we compared to the WMT07 gold standard using Bleu (Papineni et al., 2002).

H05-1117 12 51:168 3 Previous Work The idea of employing n-gram co-occurrence statistics to score the output of a computer system against one or more desired reference outputs was first successfully implemented in the BLEU metric for machine translation (Papineni et al. , 2002).

P07-1091 13 135:196 (Case-sensitive) BLEU-4 (Papineni et al. , 2002) is used as the evaluation metric.

W07-0704 14 71:182 We employ the phrase-based SMT framework (Koehn et al. , 2003), and use the Moses toolkit (Koehn et al. , 2007), and the SRILM language modelling toolkit (Stolcke, 2002), and evaluate our decoded translations using the BLEU measure (Papineni et al. , 2002), using a single reference translation.

Figure 6: Snapshot of the citation summary for a paper

The citation text that we have extracted for each paper is a good resource to generate summaries of the contributions of that paper. We have previously developed systems using clustering the similarity networks to generate short, and yet informative, summaries of individual papers (Qazvinian and Radev 2008), and more general scientific topics, such as Dependency Parsing, and Machine Translation (Radev et al. 2009) .

7 Gender annotation

We have manually annotated the gender of most authors in AAN using the name of the author. If the gender cannot be identified without any ambiguity using the name of the author, we resorted to finding the homepage of the author. We have been able to annotate 8,578 authors this way: 6,396 male and 2,182 female.

8 Downloads

The following files can be downloaded:

Text files of the paper: The raw text files of the papers after converting them from pdf to text is available for all papers. The files are named by the corresponding ACL ID.

Metadata: This file contains all the metadata associated with each paper. The metadata associated with every paper consists of the paper id, title, year, venue.

Citations: The paper citation network indicating which paper cites which other paper.

Figure 7 includes some examples.

id = {C98-1096}
author = {Jing, Hongyan; McKeown, Kathleen R.}
title = {Combining Multiple, Large-Scale Resources in a Reusable Lexicon for Natural Language Generation}
venue = {International Conference On Computational Linguistics}
year = {1998}

id = {J82-3004}
author = {Church, Kenneth Ward; Patil, Ramesh}
title = {Coping With Syntactic Ambiguity Or How To Put The Block In The Box On The Table}
venue = {American Journal Of Computational Linguistics}
year = {1982}

```
A00-1001 ==> J82-3002
A00-1002 ==> C90-3057
C08-1001 ==> N06-1007
C08-1001 ==> N06-1008
```

Figure 7: Sample contents of the downloadable corpus

We also include a large set of scripts which use the paper citation network and the metadata file to output the auxiliary networks and the different statistics.

The scripts are documented here: http://clair.si.umich.edu/ .The data set has already been downloaded from 2,775 unique IPs since June 2007. Also, the website has been very popular based on access statistics. There have been more than 2M accesses in 2009.

References

Vahed Qazvinian and Dragomir R. Radev. Scientific paper summarization using citation summary networks. In COLING 2008, Manchester, UK, 2008.

Dragomir R. Radev, Mark Joseph, Bryan Gibson, and Pradeep Muthukrishnan. A Bibliometric and Network Analysis of the Field of Computational Linguistics. JASIST, 2009 to appear.

NLP Support for Faceted Navigation in Scholarly Collections

Marti A. Hearst
School of Information, UC Berkeley
102 South Hall, Berkeley, CA 94720
hearst@ischool.berkeley.edu

Emilia Stoica
Ask.com
555 12th Street, Oakland, CA 94607
emilia.stoica@ask.com

Abstract

Hierarchical faceted metadata is a proven and popular approach to organizing information for navigation of information collections. More recently, digital libraries have begun to adopt faceted navigation for collections of scholarly holdings. A key impediment to further adoption is the need for the creation of subject-oriented faceted metadata. The Castanet algorithm was developed for the purpose of (semi) automated creation of such structures. This paper describes the application of Castanet to journal title content, and presents an evaluation suggesting its efficacy. This is followed by a discussion of areas for future work.

1 Introduction

Faceted navigation for searching and browsing "vertical" content collections has become the standard interface paradigm for e-commerce shopping web sites. Faceted navigation, when properly designed, has been shown to be understood by users and preferred over other organizations (Hearst et al., 2002; Yee et al., 2003; English et al., 2001). Although text clustering is an easily automated technique, numerous studies have found that the results of clustering are difficult for lay people to understand (Kleiboemer et al., 1996; Russell et al., 2006; Hornbæk and Frøkjær, 1999) and that the coherent and predictable structure of categorical metadata is superior from a usability prespective (Rodden et al., 2001; Pratt et al., 1999; Hearst, 2006a).

An interface using hierarchical faceted navigation simultaneously shows previews of where to go next and how to return to previous states in the exploration, while seamlessly integrating free text search within the category structure. Faceted metadata provides organizing context for results and for subsequent queries, which can act as important scaffolding for exploration and discovery. The mental work of searching an information collection is reduced by promoting recognition over recall and suggesting logical but perhaps unexpected alternatives, while at the same time avoiding empty results sets.

Recently, faceted navigation has emerged as the dominant method for new interfaces for navigating digital library collections. The NCSU library catalog was an early adopter among university libraries, using the Endeca product as its backend (Antelman et al., 2006). A usability study with 10 undergraduates comparing this system to the old library catalog interface found a 48% improvement in task completion time, although the study did not account for the effects of facets vs. the effects of fuller coverage in the keyword search.

Additionally, a consortium of university libraries (the OCLC) is now using the WorldCat shared catalog and interface, which features a faceted navigation component (see Figures 1 and 2). And another popular interface solution is provided by AquaBrowser, in this case, shown on the University of Chicago website (see Figure 3). A recent study on this site found significant benefits attributable to the faceted navigation facility (Olson, 2007). And finally, the online citation system DBLP has not one but two different faceted interfaces, as does the ACM Digital Library.

These interfaces do a good job of allowing users to filter by bibliographic attributes such as media, date, and library. However, in most cases the subject metadata still is not as rich as it should be to fully facilitate information browsing and discovery in these systems. In fact, there are a number of open problems with the use of faceted navigation for scholarly work. Some of these have to do with how best to present faceted navigation in the interface (Hearst, 2006b), but others are more relevant

Proceedings of the 2009 Workshop on Text and Citation Analysis for Scholarly Digital Libraries, ACL-IJCNLP 2009, pages 62–70, Suntec, Singapore, 7 August 2009.

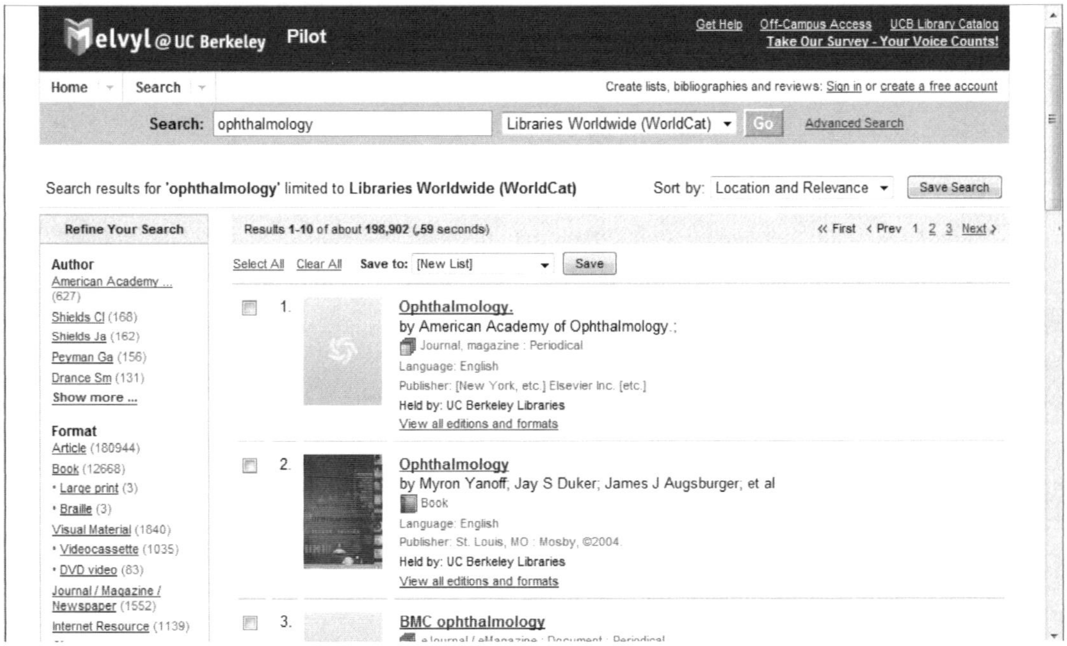

Figure 1: Worldcat consortium digital library interface using faceted navigation. The instance shown is the University of California version, from http://berkeley.worldcat.org .

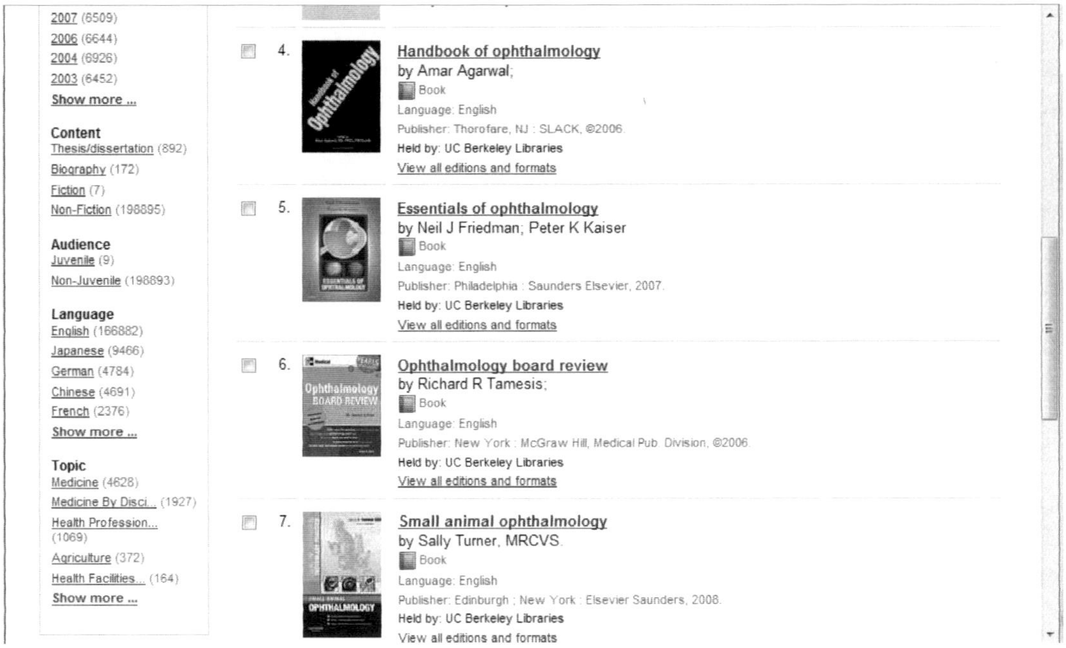

Figure 2: Digital library interface with faceted navigation, continued, from http://berkeley.worldcat.org .

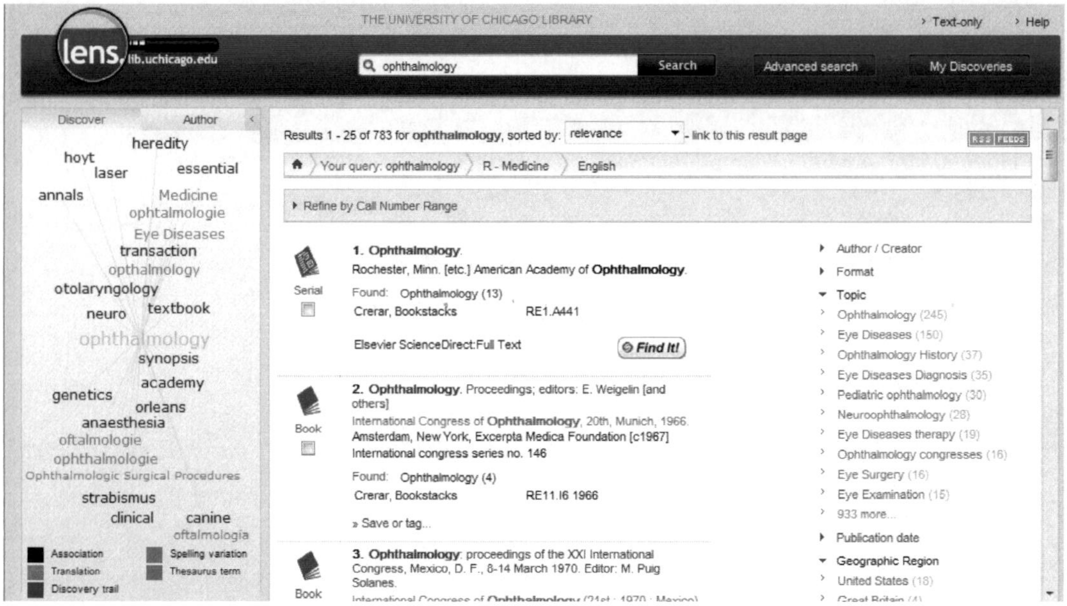

Figure 3: University of Chicago digital library interface using faceted navigation, using an interface from AquaBrowser.

to NLP, including:

- How to automatically or semi-automatically create rich subject-oriented faceted metadata for scholarly text?
- How to automatically assign information items to faceted category labels?

This paper describes the results of applying Castanet, a semi-automated approach to creating faceted metadata, to a scholarly collection. (In past work it has been shown to work well on a different kind of text (Stoica et al., 2007; Stoica and Hearst, 2004).) It then discusses some open problems in building navigation structures for scholarly digital libraries.

2 Creating Faceted Metadata

This section first defines faceted metadata, and then describes the CastaNet algorithm. More details about the algorithm can be found in a prior publication (Stoica et al., 2007).

Rather than one large category hierarchy, faceted metadata consists of a set of categories (flat or hierarchical), each of which corresponds to a different facet (dimension or feature type) relevant to the collection to be navigated. After the facets are designed, each item in the collection is assigned any number of labels from the facets.

Faceted metadata is intermediate in complexity between flat categories and full knowledge representation. The idea is to develop a set of "orthogonal" categories that characterize the information space in a meaningful way, using terminology that is useful for browsing the contents of a domain. Each facet is a different topic, subject, attribute, or feature, and some facets have hierarchical "is-a" structure. For instance, the facets of a biomedical collection should cover disease, anatomy, drugs, symptoms, side-effects, properties of experimental subjects, and so on. Each biomedical article can then be assigned any number of category labels from any number of facets. An article on the effects of tamoxifen on ovarian cancer when tested on mice could then be navigated to by first starting with cancer, then selecting drug tamoxifen, and then body part ovary, or first with tamoxifen, then navigating to ovary, and further refining by disease type. This ability to "mix and match" both for describing the articles and for navigating the category structure is key.

The term "faceted classification" was deliberately chosen in the Flamenco project to echo the old library science term of that name (Hearst, 2000), but with a rejection of the strict terms required for construction of controlled vocabulary, which mandates exhaustive, mutually exclusive category composition. Rather, the faceted navigation approach for design of search interfaces calls for category systems that are expressed at a meaningful level of description, use approachable language (unless designed for specialists), are consistent in terms of specificity at each level, avoiding becoming too broad or too deep.

The most difficult part of the design is determining whether or not compound concepts should be created. For instance, when evaluating tags for a digital library like librarything, should terms like "african history" and "british literature" be separated into two facets, one containing major writing types (history, literature), and another nationalities (african, british), or should the modifying structure be retained, as there are many kinds of history and many kinds of literature? Most likely, the answer should depend on the makeup of the collection and the usage that the users are expected to want to make of it.

The next subsections briefly describe related work in automated creation of structure from text, the Castanet algorithm and its output on journal article title text, and the results of a usability study on this output.

2.1 Related Work

One way to create faceted metadata is to start with existing vocabularies, and in fact work has been done on this area. The Library of Congress Subject headings are shown in the U Chicago catalog, despite a statement by Antelman et al. (2006) about the "unsuitability of Library of Congress Subject Headings (LCSH) as an entry vocabulary." There has also been work on converting LCSH into faceted metadata (Anderson and Hofmann, 2006). Work on the Flamenco project converted the Art and Architecture thesaurus to a faceted category system manually (Hearst et al., 2002). However, automated techniques are desirable.

Other methods that are influential but claimed to make a meaningful category structure, but not necessarily a faceted one, include the LDA (Latent Dirichlet Allocation) method (Blei et al., 2003), which uses a generative probabilistic model of discrete data to create a model of documents' topics. It attempts to analyze a text corpus and extract the topics that combine to form the documents. The output of the algorithm was originally evaluated in terms of perplexity reduction but not in terms of understandability of the topics produced.

Sanderson and Croft (1999) propose a method called Subsumption for building a hierarchy for a set of documents retrieved for a query. For two terms x and y, x is said to subsume y if the following conditions hold: $P(x|y) \geq 0.8, P(y|x) < 1$. To evaluate the algorithm the authors asked 8 participants to look at parent-child pairs and state whether or not they were "interesting." Participants found 67% to be interesting as compared to 51% for randomly chosen pairs of words. Of those interesting pairs, 72% were found to display a "type-of" relationship.

Another class of solutions make use of existing lexical hierarchies to build category hierarchies, as we do in this paper. For example, Navigli and Velardi (2003) use WordNet (Fellbaum, 1998) to build a complex ontology consisting of a wide range of relation types (demonstrated on a travel agent domain), as opposed to a set of human-readable hierarchical facets. Mihalcea and Moldovan (2001) describe a sophisticated method for simplifying WordNet in general, rather than tailoring it to a specific collection.

Zelevinsky et al. (2008) used an approach of looking at keywords assigned by authors of ACM publications to documents, computing which terms had high importance within those documents, and then using the highest scoring among those documents to assign new keywords (referred to in the paper as tags) to the documents. The tags were shown as query term refinements in a digital library interface.

Only limited related work has attempted to make faceted category hierarchies explicitly. Dakka et al. (Dakka and Ipeirotis, 2008; Dakka et al., 2005) is one of these. Their approach is a combination of Subsumption and Castanet; they use lexical resources like WordNet and Wikipedia to find structure among words, but also use them to determine which words in a collection are most useful to include in a faceted system. The facet hierarchy is made via Subsumption. The evaluation of their most recent work on news text finds strong results for assessments made by judges of precision and recall. Furthermore, when facets were shown in a search interface to five users, the keyword usage dropped in favor of clicking on categories, as task completion time was reduced while satisfaction remained unchanged. No examples of facet categories produced by the algorithm are shown, and the role of hierarchy is not clear, but the approach appears especially promising for determining which words of long documents to include in building facet systems.

2.2 Castanet Applied to Journal Titles

The main idea behind the Castanet algorithm is to carve out a structure from the hypernym ("is-a") relations within the WordNet (Fellbaum, 1998) lexical database (Stoica et al., 2007; Stoica and Hearst, 2004). The Castanet algorithm assumes that there is text associated with each item in the collection, or at least with a representative subset of the items. The textual descriptions are used *both* to build the facet hierarchies and to assign items (documents, images, citations, etc.) to the facets, and the text can be fragmented.

The algorithm has five major steps which are briefly outlined here. For details, see (2007).

1. Select target terms from textual descriptions of information items.
2. Build the Core Tree:
    - For each term, if the term is unambiguous, add its synset's IS-A path to the Core Tree.
    - Increment the counts for each node in the synset's path with the number of documents in which the target term appears.
3. Augment the Core Tree with the remaining terms' paths:
    - For each candidate IS-A path for the ambiguous term, choose the path for which there is the most document representation in the Core Tree.
4. Compress the augmented tree.
5. Remove top-level categories, yielding a set of facet hierarchies.

In addition to augmenting the nodes in the tree, adding in a new term increases a count associated with each node on its path; this count corresponds to how many documents the term occurs in. Thus the more common a term, the more weight it places on the path it falls within. The Core Tree acts as the "backbone" for the final category structure. It is built by using paths derived from unambiguous terms, with the goal of biasing the final structure towards the appropriate senses of words. Currently a word can appear in only one sense in the final structure; allowing multiple senses is an area of research.

Figures 4 and 5 show the output of the Castanet algorithm when applied to the titles of journals from the bioscience literature. Note that even the highly ambiguous common anatomy words are successfully grouped using this algorithm, presumably because of the requirement that each word occur in only one location in the ontology and because the anatomy part of the ontology is strongly favored during the part of the process in which the core tree is built with unambiguous terms. (Although some versions of Castanet use an advanced version of WordNet Domains (Magnini, 2000), they were not used in the construction of this category set.)

As reported earlier (Stoica et al., 2007), an evaluation of this algorithm was conducted by asking information architects with expertise in the domain over which the algorithm was run to state whether or not they would like to use the output of the algorithm to build a website. The output of Castanet was compared to Subsumption (Sanderson and Croft, 1999) and to LDA (Blei et al., 2003).

As reported earlier, on a recipes collection, all 34 information architects overwhelming preferred Castanet. They were asked to respond to how likely they would be to use the output, on a scale of: definitely no, no, yes, definitely yes. For Castanet, 85% of the evaluators said yes or definitely yes for intent to use. Subsumption received 38% answering yes or definitely yes, and LDA was rejected by all participants.

The study was also conducted using a biological journal titles collection. 3275 titles were used (although a significant number are not in English and so many are missed by the algorithm). The 15 participants who evaluated the Biomedical titles collection were required to be frequent users of PubMed (the online library for biomedicine), but were not required to be information architects, as it was difficult to finding information architects with biological expertise. These participants were biologists, doctors, medical students and medical librarians.

7 participants saw both LDA and Castanet, and 8 participants saw both Subsumption and Castanet (a pilot test found that participants who saw both Subsumption and LDA became very frustrated with the tasks, so the two options were compared pairwise to Castanet for subsequent trials). For Castanet, 11 out of 15 participants (73%) an-

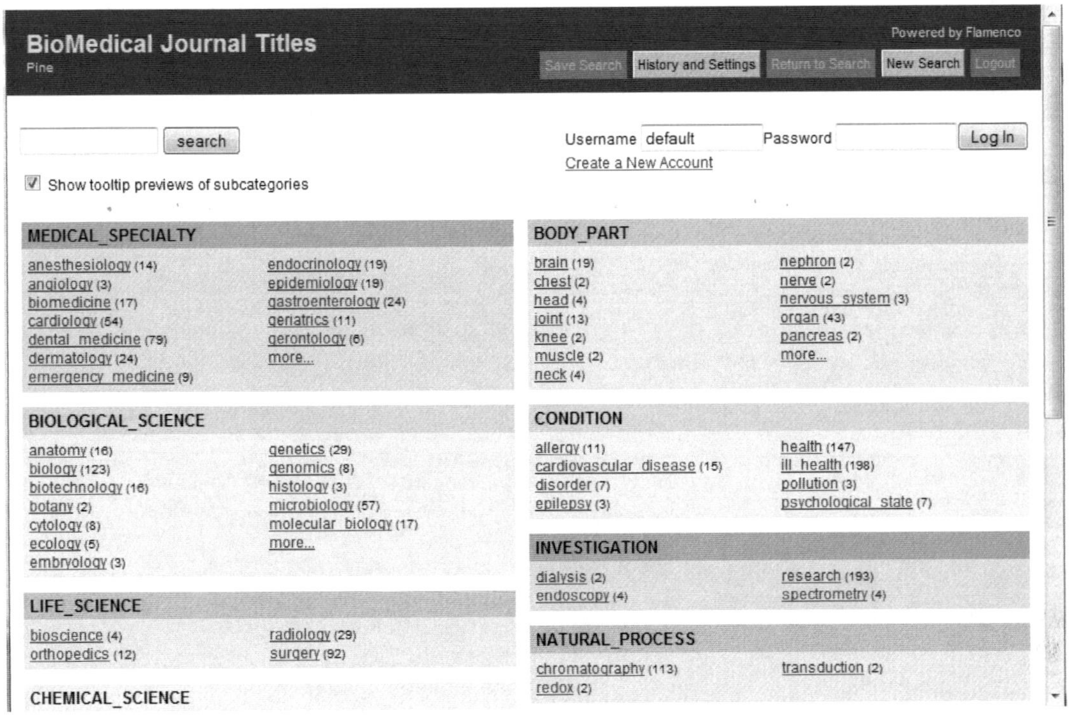

Figure 4: Castanet output on journal title text.

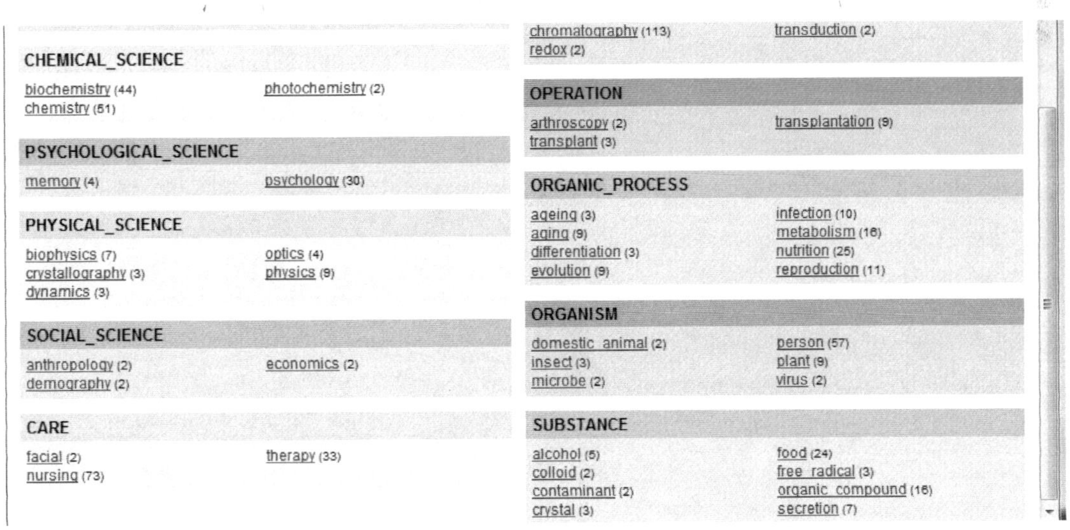

Figure 5: Castanet output on journal title text, continued.

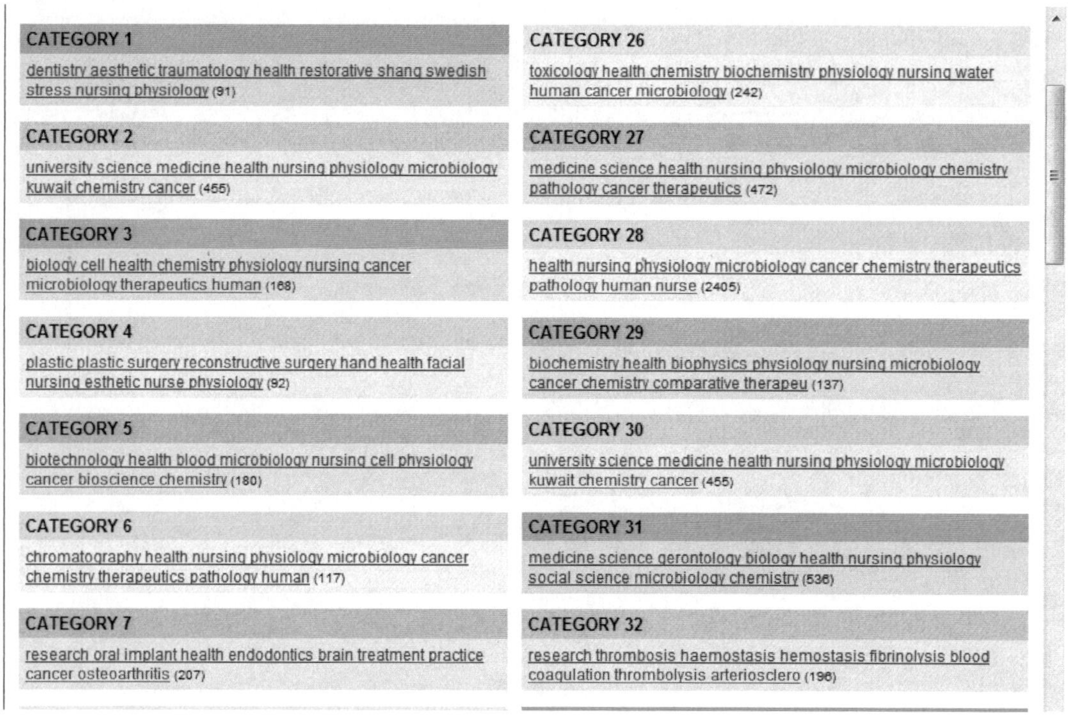

Figure 6: LDA output on journal title text.

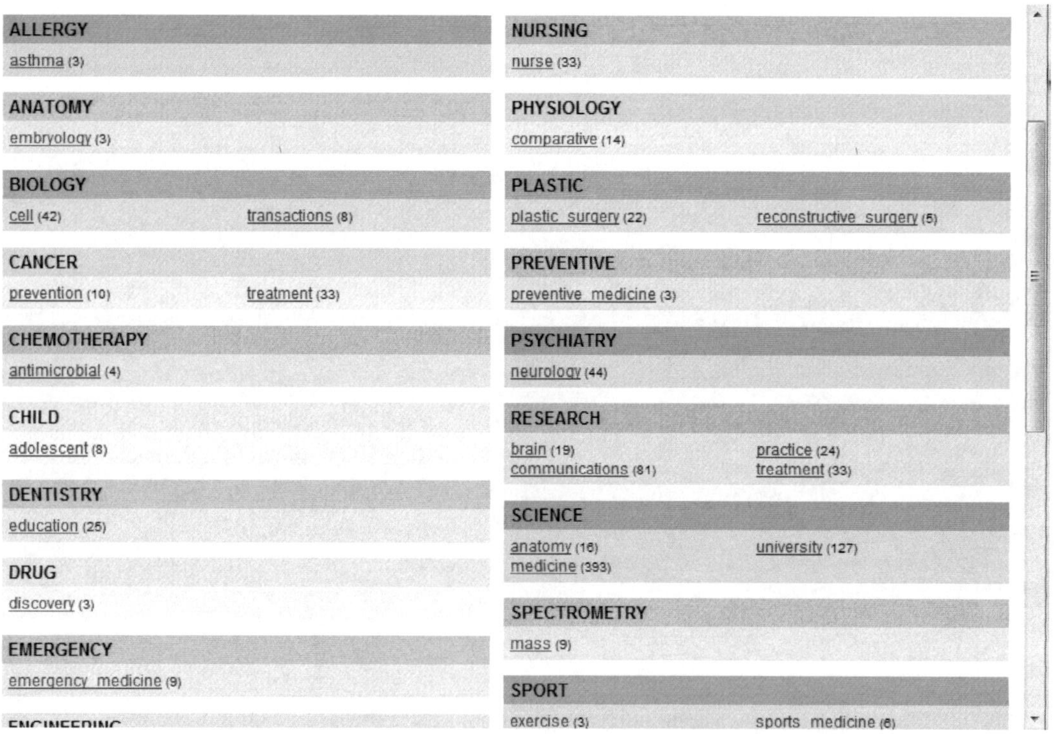

Figure 7: Subsumption output on journal title text.

swered yes or definitely yes to a desire to use its output. 1 out of 7 participants answered yes to a desire to use LDA, and 1 out of 8 answered yes to Subsumption. LDA received 4 "definitely no" responses, whereas Subsumption received only one of these, and no one said definitely no to Castanet.

2.3 Open Problems

Although quite useful "out of the box," the Castanet algorithm could benefit by several improvements and additions:

1. The processing of the terms should recognize spelling variations (such as aging vs. ageing) and morphological variations. Verbs and adjectives are often quite important for a collection and should be included, but with caution.
2. In a related point, the system should have a way of suggesting synonyms to annotate a given node, as opposed to listing closely related words as children or siblings of one another.
3. Some terms should be allowed to occur with more than one sense if this is required by the dataset. For example, the term *brain* is annotated with two domains, *Anatomy* and *Psychology*, which are both relevant domains for a biomedical journal collection.
4. Words that appear in noun compounds and phrases that are not in WordNet should receive special processing.
5. Currently if a term is in a document it is assumed to use the sense assigned in the facet hierarchies; this is often incorrect, and so terms should be disambiguated within the text before automatic category assignment is done.
6. WordNet is not exhaustive and some mechanism is needed to improve coverage for unknown terms.
7. Castanet seems to work better when applied to short pieces of text (e.g., journal titles vs. full text); to remedy this, better methods are needed to select the target terms.
8. A method for dynamically adding facets and adding terms to facets should be developed, especially a method for allowing user tags to be incorporated into the exising facet hierarchies.

Recent work by Dakka et al. (Dakka and Ipeirotis, 2008) can help with point 7, and some recent work by Koren et al. (Koren et al., 2008) seems promising for 8.

Robust evaluation methods are also needed; making use of log information about which facets are heavily used can help inform decisions about which facets work well and which need modification or additions.

Acknowledgements: Megan Richardson provided valuable contributions in her work on the study reported on here. Emilia Stoica did this work while a postdoctoral researcher at UC Berkeley.

References

J.D. Anderson and M.A. Hofmann. 2006. A fully faceted syntax for Library of Congress subject headings. *Cataloging & Classification Quarterly*, 43(1):7–38.

K. Antelman, E. Lynema, and A.K. Pace. 2006. Toward a twenty-first century library catalog. *Information technology and libraries*, 25(3):128–138.

David Blei, Andrew Y. Ng, and Michael I. Jordan. 2003. Latent dirichlet allocation. *Journal of Machine Learning Research*, 3:993–1022.

W. Dakka and P.G. Ipeirotis. 2008. Automatic extraction of useful facet hierarchies from text databases. In *IEEE 24th International Conference on Data Engineering, 2008. ICDE 2008*, pages 466–475.

W. Dakka, P.G. Ipeirotis, and K.R. Wood. 2005. Automatic construction of multifaceted browsing interfaces. In *Proceedings of the 14th ACM international conference on Information and knowledge management*, pages 768–775. ACM New York, NY, USA.

J. English, M.A. Hearst, R. Sinha, K. Swearingen, and K.-P. Yee. 2001. Examining the usability of web site search. Unpublished Manuscript, http://flamenco.berkley.edu/papers/epicurious-study.pdf.

Christiane Fellbaum, editor. 1998. *WordNet: An Electronic Lexical Database*. MIT Press.

M.A. Hearst, J. English, R. Sinha, K. Swearingen, and K.-P. Yee. 2002. Finding the flow in web site search. *Communications of the ACM*, 45(9), September.

M.A. Hearst. 2000. Next Generation Web Search: Setting Our Sites. *IEEE Data Engineering Bulletin*, 23(3):38–48.

M.A. Hearst. 2006a. Clustering Versus Faceted Categories For Information Exploration. *Communcations Of The Acm*, 49(4):59–61.

M.A. Hearst. 2006b. Design recommendations for hierarchical faceted search interfaces. In *SIGIR'06 Workshop On Faceted Search*, Seattle, Wa, August.

K. Hornbæk and E. Frøkjær. 1999. Do Thematic Maps Improve Information Retrieval. *Human-Computer Interaction (INTERACT'99)*, pages 179–186.

A.J. Kleiboemer, M.B. Lazear, and J.O. Pedersen. 1996. Tailoring a retrieval system for naive users. In *Proceedings of the Fifth Annual Symposium on Document Analysis and Information Retrieval (SDAIR '96)*, Las Vegas, NV.

J. Koren, Y. Zhang, and X. Liu. 2008. Personalized interactive faceted search. *WWW '08: Proceeding of the 17th international conference on World Wide Web*.

Bernardo Magnini. 2000. Integrating subject field codes into WordNet. In *Proc. of LREC 2000*, Athens, Greece.

Rada Mihalcea and Dan I. Moldovan. 2001. Ez.wordnet: Principles for automatic generation of a coarse grained wordnet. In *Proc. of FLAIRS Conference 2001*, May.

Roberto Navigli, Paola Velardi, and Aldo Gangemi. 2003. Ontology learning and its application to automated terminology translation. *Intelligent Systems*, 18(1):22–31.

T.A. Olson. 2007. Utility of a faceted catalog for scholarly research. *Library Hi Tech*, 25(4):550–561.

W. Pratt, M.A. Hearst, and L. Fagan. 1999. A knowledge-based approach to organizing retrieved documents. In *Proceedings of 16th Annual Conference on Artificial Intelligence(AAAI 99)*, Orlando, FL.

K. Rodden, W. Basalaj, D. Sinclair, and K. R. Wood. 2001. Does organisation by similarity assist image browsing? In *Proceeedings of ACM CHI 2001*, pages 190–197.

D.M. Russell, M. Slaney, Y. Qu, and M. Houston. 2006. Being literate with large document collections: Observational studies and cost structure tradeoffs. In *Proceedings of the 39th Annual Hawaii International Conference on System Sciences (HICSS'06)*.

Mark Sanderson and Bruce Croft. 1999. Deriving concept hierarchies from text. In *Proceedings of SIGIR 1999*.

E. Stoica and M. Hearst. 2004. Nearly-automated metadata hierarchy creation. In *Companion Proceedings of HLT-NAACL'04*, pages 117–120.

E. Stoica, M.A. Hearst, and M. Richardson. 2007. Automating Creation of Hierarchical Faceted Metadata Structures. In *Human Language Technologies: The Annual Conference of the North American Chapter of the Association for Computational Linguistics (NAACL-HLT 2007)*, pages 244–251.

K.-P. Yee, K. Swearingen, K. Li, and M.A. Hearst. 2003. Faceted metadata for image search and browsing. In *Proceedings of ACM CHI 2003*, pages 401–408. ACM New York, NY, USA.

V. Zelevinsky, J. Wang, and D. Tunkelang. 2008. Supporting Exploratory Search for the ACM Digital Library. In *Workshop on Human-Computer Interaction and Information Retrieval (HCIR'08)*.

FireCite: Lightweight real-time reference string extraction from webpages

Ching Hoi Andy Hong **Jesse Prabawa Gozali** **Min-Yen Kan**
School of Computing
National University of Singapore
{hongchin,jprabawa,kanmy}@comp.nus.edu.sg

Abstract

We present FireCite, a Mozilla Firefox browser extension that helps scholars assess and manage scholarly references on the web by automatically detecting and parsing such reference strings in real-time. FireCite has two main components: 1) a reference string recognizer that has a high recall of 96%, and 2) a reference string parser that can process HTML web pages with an overall F_1 of .878 and plaintext reference strings with an overall F_1 of .97. In our preliminary evaluation, we presented our FireCite prototype to four academics in separate unstructured interviews. Their positive feedback gives evidence to the desirability of FireCite's citation management capabilities.

1 Introduction

On the Web, many web pages like researchers' or conference homepages contain references to academic papers much like citations in a bibliography. These references do not always follow a specific reference style. Usually, they make use of HTML formatting to differentiate fields and emphasize keywords. For example in Figure 1, paper titles are displayed in bold.

Depending on personal preference and habit, references found on the Web may be processed in various ways. This process however, can possibly be quite a long chain of events:

1. A researcher finds a PDF copy of the paper and downloads it.
2. He reads the abstract of the paper, then decides to read the rest of it.
3. He prints out the paper and reads it, making annotations along the margin as he reads.
4. He produces a BibTeX entry for the paper.

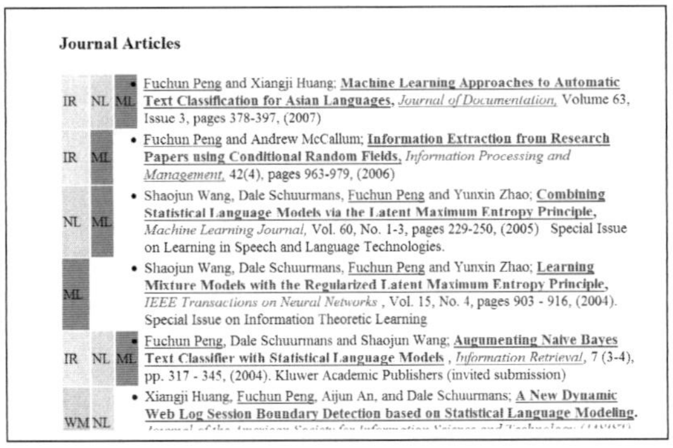

Figure 1: A web page with a list of references. Paper titles are displayed in **bold**.

5. He cites the paper in his own work.

This process is too time-consuming for researchers to do for each reference, one at a time. One solution is to collect all the references of interest first. These references can then be processed at a later time. Bibliographic Management Applications (BMAs) do exactly this by allowing the researcher to record interesting references for later use. Alternatively, the references can be recorded manually on paper or in a text file. The paper for each reference can also be printed and organized physically in folders or piles.

Each method has its own disadvantages. Using notebooks, text files or printouts imposes considerable cognitive load on the researcher especially when hundreds of references need to be managed. BMAs seek to relieve researchers from this problem, but are often too complicated to use and maintain. A popular BMA, EndNote, for example, retrieves metadata from online library catalogues and databases, but experience is necessary to know which database or catalogue to search. Considerable time can be lost searching for a computer science paper in a medical database. An automatic, yet lightweight solution is needed.

Since the references are found on the Web, the most suitable location for a BMA is within the web

Proceedings of the 2009 Workshop on Text and Citation Analysis for Scholarly Digital Libraries, ACL-IJCNLP 2009, pages 71–79, Suntec, Singapore, 7 August 2009.

browser itself. In this paper, we propose FireCite[1], a Firefox browser extension which embodies this idea. FireCite 1) automatically recognizes references on web pages, 2) parses these references into title, authors, and date fields, 3) allows the researcher to save these references for later use, and 4) allows a local PDF copy of the paper to be saved for each reference.

At its core, FireCite consists of a reference string recognizer and a reference string parser with accuracies comparable to other systems. Unlike these systems however, as a browser extension, FireCite needs to be fast and lightweight. Bloated extensions can cause the browser's memory footprint to grow significantly, lowering overall performance. An extension must also perform its operations fast. Otherwise, it will detract users from their primary task with the browser. Nah (2004) suggests latencies should be kept within two seconds.

In the next section, we review related work. We then discuss reference string recognition, followed by parsing in Section 3. After component evaluations, we conclude by discussing the user interface of FireCite.

2 Related Work

Recognizing and parsing reference strings has been a task tackled by many, as it is a necessary task in modern digital libraries.

Past work has dealt primarily with clean data, where reference strings are already delimited (e.g., in the References or Bibliography section of a scholarly work). Many works consider both reference string recognition and reference string parsing as a single combined problem. With regards to the task, IEPAD (Chang et al., 2003) looks for patterns among the HTML tags, while (Zhai and Liu, 2005) looks for patterns among the presentation features of the web page. A machine learning approach using Conditional Random Fields is also discussed in a few works (Xin et al., 2008; Zhu et al., 2006).

CRE (Yang et al., 2008) is an automatic reference string recognizer that works on publication list pages. Given such a page, CRE identifies individual reference strings by looking for contiguous common style patterns. The system is based on the authors' two observations: 1) 'reference string records are usually presented in one or more contiguous regions', and 2) 'reference string records are usually presented by using similar tag sequences and organized under a common parent node'. Therefore, the system examines the DOM[2] tree of the web page and identifies adjacent subtrees that are similar. The system then removes subtrees that are unlikely to be reference strings, by comparing their word count against a database of reference strings' word counts. The authors report an F_1 of around 90% for pages where reference strings make up at least 80% of the text on the page, and an F_1 of at least 70% when reference strings make up at least 30% of the page.

Of note is that their testing dataset consists solely of computer science researchers' homepages and publication list pages. There is no indication of how their system will perform for other types of web pages. Although there are many published works on the extraction of semi-structured data from web pages, very few of them deal directly with the issue of reference string extraction. Also, none of the works deal directly with the issue of web pages that do not contain any relevant data. In FireCite's case, this is an important issue to consider, because false positives will be parsed, and as stated previously, almost all web pages will have elements that are not part of any reference string.

As for reference string parsing, the field of Information Extraction (IE) has treated this task as one of its sample applications. As such, many different IE approaches involving different supervised classifiers have been tried.

Such classification methods require a gold standard corpus to train on. The CORA Information Extraction dataset, introduced in (Seymore et al., 1999) consists of a corpus of 500 classified reference strings extracted from computer science research papers, is used as training data. The CORA dataset is annotated with thirteen fields, including *author*, *title* and *date*.

As for classification approaches, (Hetzner, 2008; Seymore et al., 1999) and AutoBib (Geng and Yang, 2004) makes use of Hidden Markov Models (HMM), while ParsCit (Councill et al., 2008) and (Peng and McCallum, 2004) make use of Conditional Random Fields (CRF).

ParsCit's reference string parsing system makes use of CRF to learn a model that can apply meta-

[1]The latest version of the extension is at: https://addons.mozilla.org/en-US/firefox/addon/10766/

[2]Document Object Model. http://www.w3.org/DOM/

data labels to individual word tokens of a reference string. ParsCit's labeling model consists of 7 lexical features (features that make use of the meaning/category of a word, such as whether the word is a place, a month, or a first name) and 16 local and contextual features (features that makes use of formatting information about the current and neighbouring tokens, such as whether the word is in all caps). Its lexical features require the use of an extensive dictionary of names, places, publishers and months. ParsCit achieves an overall field-level F_1 of .94.

Another competitive method, FLUX-CiM (Cortez et al., 2007) also parses plain-text reference strings, based on a knowledge base of reference strings. Initially, labels are assigned to tokens based on the (label, token) pair's likelihood of appearance in the knowlege base. For tokens that do not occur in the knowledge base, a binding step is used to associate them with neighbouring tokens that have already been labelled. The authors report a very high token-level accuracy in terms of F_1 of 98.4% for reference strings in the Computer Science (CS) domain, and 97.4% for reference strings in the Health Sciences domain.

A key difference from other parsing methods is that tokens in FLUX-CiM are strings delimited by punctuation rather than single words (see an example in Figure 2). This comes from an observation by the authors that "in general, in a reference string, every field value is bounded by a delimiter, but not all delimiters bound a field."

[Atlas], [L]., [and S]. [Shamma],
"[Joint Acoustic and Modulation Frequency],"
[EURASIP JASP], [2003].

Figure 2: A tokenised reference string. Each box contains one token.

While both ParsCit and FLUX-CiM have high levels of performance, they are not suitable for our use for two reasons:

- Both systems are large. ParsCit's classifier model plus dictionaries add up to about 10MB. FLUX-CiM requires a database of 3000 reference strings for each knowledge domain, for best performance. Databases of this size will take a significant amount of time to load and to access, negatively impacting the user experience.
- Both systems are not designed to handle web reference strings. Neither system is able to correctly parse a reference string such as the one shown in Figure 3 due to its lack of punctuation and the misleading tokens that resemble publication dates.

Doe, J. 2000 **1942-1945: World War Two and its effects on economy and technology.** Generic Publisher. Generic Country.

Figure 3: A reference string that FLUX-CiM and ParsCit cannot parse correctly.

3 Methodology

FireCite performs its task of reference extraction in two logically separate stages: recognition and parsing. Reference string recognition locates and delimits the start and end of reference strings on a web page, while parsing delimits the internal fields within a recognized reference.

3.1 Recognition

Reference recognition itself can be logically segmented into two tasks: deciding whether references could occur on a page; and if so, delimiting the individual reference strings. We build a rough filter for the first task, and solve the second task using a three stage heuristic cascade.

Algorithm 1 Reference recognition.

1: Exclude pages based on URL and absence of keywords
2: Split token stream into a set S of (non-overlapping) sequences, where each sequence contains at most one reference string, and no reference string is split across two token sequences.
3: Select sequences likely to be reference strings, forming a set S' which is parsed into a set of reference strings C.
4: Remove sequences with nonsensical parse results from the set of reference strings C.

We now detail these stages.

Stage 1 immediately discards webpages that do not meet three criteria from subsequent automatic processing. For a page to be automatically processed by subsequent recognition and parsing phases, FireCite requires that the webpage:

- Is from a .edu, .org, or .ac domain. Domains with country identifiers, such as www.monash.edu.au, are also accepted;

- Contains one or more of the words 'Publications', 'Readings', 'Citations', 'Papers', and 'References'.

- Contains one or more of the words 'Conference', 'Academic', 'Journal', and 'Research'.

The included domains include web pages from academic institutions, digital libraries such as CiteseerX [3] and ACM Portal [4], and online encyclopedias such as Wikipedia [5] – basically, web pages where reference strings are likely to be found. The keywords serve to further filter away pages unlikely to contain lists of reference strings, by requiring words that are likely to appear in the headings of such lists.

Stage 1 runs very quickly and filters most non-scholarly web pages away from the subsequent, more expensive processing. This is crucial in improving the extension's efficiency, and ensuring that the extension does not incur significant latency for normal browsing activity.

Stage 2 splits the web page text into distinct chunks. In plain-text documents, we differentiate chunks by the use of blank lines. In HTML web pages, we use formatting tags: `<p>` and `<br>`. Other tags might also indicate a fresh chunk within ordered (`<ol>`) and unordered (`<ul>`) lists, list items are marked by the `<li>` tag. A horizontal rule (`<hr>`) is used to separate sections in the web page. Stage 2 makes use of all these HTML tags to split the web page text into distinct, non-overlapping sequences.

Stage 3 removes sequences that are unlikely to be reference strings, based on their length. Sequences that are too long or short are removed (i.e., with word length $5 < wl < 64$, and token lengths $4 < tl < 48$). These limits are based on the maximum and minimum word and token lengths of reference strings in the CORA corpus.

The sequences that survive this stage are sent to the parsing system, discussed in the next subsection to be parsed.

Stage 4 further removes sequences that are ill-formed. We require that all reference strings include a title and a list of authors after being parsed. Sequences that do not meet these requirements are discarded. Remaining sequences are accepted as valid reference strings.

3.2 Parsing

Between Steps 3 and 4 in the recognition process, a reference string is parsed into fields. We treat this problem as a standard classification problem for which a supervised machine learning algorithm can be trained to perform. In implementing our parsing algorithm, recall that we have to meet the criterion of a lightweight solution, which heavily influenced the resulting design.

While a full-fledged reference string parser will extract all available metadata from the reference string, including fields such as publisher name, publisher address and page numbers, we consciously designed our parser to only extract three fields: the title, the authors, and the date of publication. All other tokens are classified as Miscellaneous. There are two reasons for this: 1) for the purposes of sorting the reference strings and subsequently searching for them, these three fields are most likely to be used; 2) restricting classification space to four classes also simplifies the solution, shrinking the model size.

Another simplification was to use a decision tree classifier, as 1) the trained model is easily coded in any declarative programming language (including Javascript, the programming language used by Firefox extensions), and 2) classification is computationally inexpensive, consisting of a series of conditional statements.

Also, instead of the common practice of tokenising a string into individual words, we follow FLUX-CiM's design and use punctuation (except for hyphens and apostrophes) and HTML tags as token delimiters (as seen in the example in Figure 2). This tokenization scheme often leads to phrases. There are a few advantages to this style of tokenisation: 1) considering multiple words as a token allows more complex features to be used, thus giving a better chance of making a correct classification; and 2) reducing the number of tokens per reference string reduces the computational cost of this task.

To classify each phrase, we compile a set of ten features for use in the decision tree, comprising: 1) Lexical (dictionary) features that contain information about the meaning of the words within the token; 2) Local features that contain non-lexical

[3]hosted at http://citeseerx.ist.psu.edu
[4]http://portal.acm.org
[5]www.wikipedia.org

Feature Name	Description
PfieldLabel (*String*)	The label of the previous token
hasNumber (*Boolean*)	Whether the token contains any numbers
hasYear (*Boolean*)	Whether the token contains any 4-digit number between 1940 and 2040
fieldLength (*Integer*)	The number of characters the token has
hasMonth (*Boolean*)	Whether the token contains any month words (e.g. '**January**', '**Jan**')
oneCap (*Boolean*)	Whether the token consists of only one capital letter e.g. 'B'
position (*Float*)	A number between 0 and 1 that indicates the relative position of the token in the reference string.
hasAbbreviation (*Boolean*)	Whether the token contains any words with more than one capital letter. Examples are 'JCDL', and 'ParsCit'
startPunctuation (*String*)	The punctuation that preceded this token. Accepted values are *period, comma, hyphen, double quotes, opening brace, closing brace, colon, others,* and *none*
endPunctuation (*String*)	The punctuation that is immediately after this token. Accepted values are the same as for startPunctuation

Table 1: List of classifier features

information about the token; 3) Contextual features, which are lexical or local features of a token's neighbours. Table 1 gives an exhaustive list of features used in FireCite.

We had to exclude lexical features that require a large dictionary, such as place names and first names, as such features would add significantly to the loading and execution times of FireCite.

FireCite uses its trained model to tag input phrases with their output class. Before accepting the classification results, we make one minor repair to them. The repair stems from the observation that in gold standard reference strings, both the author and title fields are contiguous. If more than one contiguous sequence of Title or Author classification labels exist, there must be a classification error. When the extension encounters such a situation, FireCite will accept the first encountered sequence as correct, and change subsequent sequences' labels to Miscellaneous (Figure 4).

The parser joins all contiguous tokens for each category into a string, and returns the set of strings as the result.

4 Evaluation

4.1 Recognition

We took faculty homepages from the domains of four universities at random, until a set of 20 homepages with reference strings and 20 homepages without reference strings were obtained. Note that these homepages were sampled from all faculties, not merely from computer science.

Tests were conducted using these 40 pages to obtain the reference string recognition algorithm's accuracy. A reference string is considered found if there exists, in the set of confirmed reference strings C, a parsed text segment c that contains the entire title as well as all the authors' names. Each parsed text segment can only be used to identify one reference string, so if any text segments contain more than one reference string, only one of those reference strings will be considered found.

Active stages	Recall	Precision	F_1
1, 2, 3, 4	96.0%	57.5%	.719
2, 3, 4	96.6%	53.6%	.689
1, 2, 4	96.3%	51.6%	.672
1, 2, 3	98.4%	40.9%	.578
1, 2	99.2%	16.1%	.278

Table 2: Results of reference string recognition over forty web pages for five variations of FireCite's reference string recognition

In order to determine the effect of each stage on overall recognition accuracy, some stages of the recognition algorithm were disabled in testing. The results are presented in Table 2. As all test pages come from university domains, all pass the first URL test. When the keyword search is deactivated, all 40 test pages pass Stage 1. Otherwise, 19 pages with reference strings and 6 pages without reference strings pass Stage 1.

The results show that disabling individual stages of the algorithm increases recall slightly, but increases the number of false positives disproportionately more. The fully-enabled algorithm strikes a balance between the number of reference strings found and the number of false positives.

From the above results, we can also see that false positives make up around 40% of the text segments that are recognised as reference strings. However, the majority of reference strings are recognised by the algorithm. In our usage scenario, our output will eventually be viewed by a human user, who will be the final judge of what is a reference string and what is not. Therefore, it is

Thuy Dung Nguyen and Min-Yen Kan /author (2007 /date) Keyphrase Extraction in Scientific Publications/title.
In Proc/misc. of International Conference on Asian Digital Libraries/~~title~~ misc (ICADL '07/misc).
Hanoi/misc, Vietnam/misc, December/misc. pp/misc. 317-326/misc.

Figure 4: An example of an incorrectly labelled (highlighted) reference string segment

Page (# of references)	Title	Authors	Date	All Tokens
A (72)	.902	.893	.988	.708
B (52)	.953	.957	.990	.960
C (29)	.684	.304	.774	.651
D (68)	.753	.968	.889	.917
E (8)	.692	.875	1.000	.889
F (45)	.847	1.000	.989	.966
Overall	.836	.916	.948	.878

Table 3: Results of FireCite reference string parsing. Performance figures given are Token F_1. Overall F_1 includes tokens classified as Miscellaneous, and is micro-averaged.

System	Title	Authors	Date	Overall
FireCite	.940	.994	.982	.979
FLUX-CiM	.974	.994	.986	.984

Table 4: Token F_1 of FireCite and FLUX-CiM.

System	Title	Authors	Date	Overall
FireCite	.92	.96	.97	.94
ParsCit	.96	.99	.97	.94
FLUX-CiM	.93	.95	.98	.97

Table 5: Field F_1 of FireCite and other reference string parsers.

more important that we have a high recall rather than high precision. In that respect, this algorithm can be said to fulfill its purpose.

4.2 Parsing

To evaluate the reference string parsing algorithm, we randomly selected six staff publication pages from a computer science faculty. The presentation of each page, as well as the presentation of reference strings on each page, were all chosen to differ from each other. There are a total of 274 reference strings in these six pages. We annotated the reference strings by hand; this set of annotations is used as the gold standard. The six pages are loaded using a browser with FireCite installed. FireCite processes each page and produces a output file with the parsed reference strings. These parsing results are then compared against the gold standard. Table 3 shows the token level results, broken down by web page.

The FireCite reference string parser is able to handle plain-text reference strings as well. A set of plain-text reference strings can be converted into a form understandable by FireCite, simply by enclosing the set of reference strings with `<html>` tags, and replacing line breaks with `<br>` tags. Table 4 shows the token F_1 of the Firecite reference string parser compared FLUX-CiM, while Table 5 shows the field F_1 of FireCite, FLUX-CiM and ParsCit. The test dataset used by all three systems is the FLUX-CiM Computer Science dataset[6] of 300 reference strings randomly selected from the ACM Digital Library. Note that in FireCite and FLUX-CiM, tokens are punctuation delimited whereas in ParsCit, tokens are word delimited.

We feel that above results show that FireCite's reference string parser is comparable to the reviewed systems (although statistically worse), despite its use of a fast and simple classifier and the lack of lexical features that require large dictionaries. The disparity of results between handling web page reference strings and handling plain-text reference strings can generally be attributed to the differences between web page reference strings and plain-text reference strings. Specifically:

- Among the testing data used, the reference strings on one web page (Page C) all begin with the title. However, in the CORA training corpus, all reference strings begin with the authors' names. As a result, in the trained classifier, the first token of every reference string is classified as 'authors'. This error is then propagated through the entire reference string, because each token makes use of the previous token's class as a classifier feature. As shown in Table 3 above, the performance for page C is much worse than the performance for the other pages.

- When web pages are created and edited using a WYSIWIG editor, such as Adobe Dreamweaver or Microsoft Office FrontPage, multiple nested and redundant HTML tags

[6] available at http://www.dcc.ufam.edu.br/ ẽccv/flux-cim/ Computer-Science/

	Min. time	Max. time	Avg. time
With references	90	544	192
W/o references	6	222	74
All pages	6	544	133

Table 6: FireCite execution time tests over 40 web pages. Times given in milliseconds.

tend to be added to the page. Because FireCite treats HTML tags as token delimiters, these redundant tags increase the number of tokens in the string, thus affecting the token position feature of the classifier, causing some tokens to become incorrectly classified.

Some of the inaccuracies can also be attributed to mistakes from reference string recognition. When the reference string is not correctly delimited, text that occurs before or after the actual reference string is also sent to the reference string parser. This affects the token position and previous token label features.

The competitive advantage of FireCite's reference string parser is that it is very small compared to the other systems. FireCite's reference string parser consists only of a decision tree coded into JavaScript if-then-else statements, and a couple of JavaScript functions, taking up a total of around 38KB of space. On the other hand, as mentioned above, FLUX-CiM optimally requires a database of around 3000 reference strings, while ParsCit's classifier model and dictionaries require a total of 10MB of space. These characteristics also make the reference string parser fast. Speed tests were conducted over 40 web pages taken from the domains of four universities, 20 of which contain reference strings and 20 of which do not. The results are summarised in Table 6. From these results we can infer with some confidence that FireCite will add no more than one second to the existing time a page takes to load.

5 Extension Front End

We thus implemented a prototype BMA as a Firefox extension that uses the recognizer and parser as core modules. As such an extension interacts with users directly, the extension's front end design concentrated on functionality and usability issues that go beyond the aforementioned natural language processing issues.

Browser extension based BMAs are not new. Zotero[7] as well as Mendeley[8] both offer BMAs that manage reference (and other bookmark) information for users. However, neither recognizes or delimits free formed reference strings found on general webpages. Both rely on predefined templates to process specific scholarly websites (e.g. Google Scholar, Springer).

In developing our front end, our design hopes to complement such existing BMAs. We followed a rapid prototyping design methodology. The current user interface, shown in Figure 5, is the result of three cycles of development. Up to now, feedback gathering has been done through focus groups with beginning research students and individual interviews with faculty members. Rather than concentrate on the design process, we give a quick synopsis of the major features that the FireCite prototype implements.

One-Click Addition of References: FireCite appends a clickable button to each reference string it detects through the recognition and parsing modules. Clicking this button adds the reference string's metadata to the reference library. The design draws attention to the presence of a reference without disrupting the layout of the webpage.

Reference Library: The reference library opens as a sidebar in the browser. It is a local database containing the metadata of the saved references. The library allows reference strings to be edited or deleted, and sorted according to the three extracted metadata fields.

Manual recognition and addition: The core modules occasionally miss valid references. To remedy this, users can manually highlight a span of text, and through the right click context menu, ask FireCite to parse the span and append an "add citation" button. The user may also manually add or edit reference metadata directly in the sidebar. This feature allows the user to add entries from his existing collections of papers, or to add entries for which no reference string can be found (such as papers that have not been published).

PDF download: When a reference is added to the local library, any Portable Document Format (PDF) file associated with the reference string is downloaded as well. Appropriate PDF files are found heuristically by finding a hyperlink leading to a PDF file within the text segment. The downloaded PDF files are stored in a single folder

[7]http://www.zotero.org
[8]http://www.mendeley.com

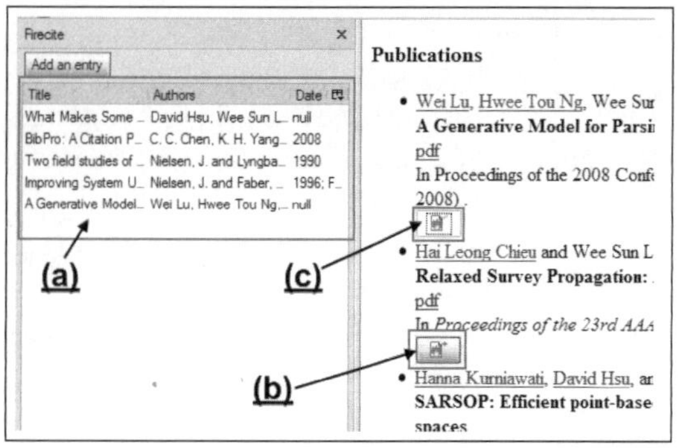

Figure 5: Screenshot of FireCite prototype illustrating (a) the reference string library, (b) button appended to each reference string, and (c) button state after the reference string has been added to the list.

within Firefox's storage location for the extension, and can be opened or deleted through the sidebar interface. With this feature, the user will not need to juggle his PDF files and reference string library separately.

As a preliminary evaluation, we presented FireCite to four academics in separate unstructured interviews. All four subjects saw the potential of FireCite as a BMA, but not the usefulness of recognising reference strings on the Web. Two of them pointed out that they rarely encounter reference strings while browsing the Web, while another only needs to search for specific, known papers. When asked in detail, it was apparent that subjects do actually visit web pages that contain many reference strings. In DBLP, each entry is actually a reference string. In the ACM Digital Library, in every article information page, there is a list of reference strings that have been extracted from the bibliography of the article using Optical Character Recognition (OCR).

From our study, we conclude that integration with template based recognition (*a la* Zotero) of sites such as DBLP, Google Scholar and ACM Portal, has better potential. As expected, since the subjects all have significant research experience, they have already developed suitable research methods. The challenge is for FireCite to fit into their workflow.

6 Conclusion

This paper describes FireCite, a Firefox extension that can recognise and delimit metadata from reference strings on freeform web pages. FireCite's

"Liquidity-Based Model of Security Design," with Darrell Duffie, Econometrica, 1999, 67, 65-99.

Figure 6: A reference string with one author's name omitted.

Michael Collins and Terry Koo.
Discriminative Reranking for Natural Language Parsing.
Computational Linguistics 31(1):25-69.

Figure 7: A reference string with its year omitted. Part of a list of reference strings organised by their year of publication.

implementation demonstrates it is possible to do these tasks in real-time and with a usable level of accuracy.

We have validated the accuracy of FireCite's embedded recognition and parsing modules by comparing against the state-of-the-art systems, both on web based reference strings that use HTML tags as well as gold-standard reference strings in plain text. FireCite achieves a usable level of reference string recognition and parsing accuracy, while remaining small in size, a critical requirement in building a browser extension. This small model allows FireCite to complete its processing of reference heavy webpages in under one second, an acceptable level of latency for most users. Preliminary user studies show that the FireCite system should incorporate template based recognition of large scholarly sites as well for maximum effectiveness.

Future work on the parsing and recognition will focus on capturing implied contextual information. On some web pages the author may omit their own name, or place the year of publication in a section head (Figures 6 and 7). We are working towards recognizing and incorporating such contextual information in processing.

Acknowledgements

This work was partially supported by a National Research Foundation grant "Interactive Media Search" (grant # R 252 000 325 279).

References

Chia-Hui Chang, Chun-Nan Hsu, and Shao-Cheng Lui. 2003. Automatic information extraction from semistructured web pages by pattern discovery. *Decis. Support Syst.*, 35(1):129–147.

Eli Cortez, Altigran S. da Silva, Marcos André Gonçalves, Filipe Mesquita, and Edleno S. de Moura. 2007. FLUX-CIM: flexible unsupervised extraction of citation metadata. In *Proc. JCDL '07*, pages 215–224, New York, NY, USA. ACM.

Isaac G. Councill, C. Lee Giles, and Min-Yen Kan. 2008. ParsCit: An open-source CRF reference string parsing package. In *LREC '08*, Marrakesh, Morrocco, May.

Junfei Geng and Jun Yang. 2004. Autobib: automatic extraction of bibliographic information on the web. pages 193–204, July.

Erik Hetzner. 2008. A simple method for citation metadata extraction using hidden markov models. In *Proc. JCDL '08*, pages 280–284, New York, NY, USA. ACM.

Fiona Fui-Hoon Nah. 2004. A study on tolerable waiting time: how long are web users willing to wait? *Behaviour & Information Technology Special Issue on HCI in MIS*, 23(3), May-June.

Fuchun Peng and Andrew McCallum. 2004. Accurate information extraction from research papers using conditional random fields. pages 329–336. HLT-NAACL.

Kristie Seymore, Andrew McCallum, and Roni Rosenfeld. 1999. Learning hidden markov model structure for information extraction. In *AAAI'99 Workshop on Machine Learning for Information Extraction*.

Xin Xin, Juanzi Li, Jie Tang, and Qiong Luo. 2008. Academic conference homepage understanding using constrained hierarchical conditional random fields. In *Proc. CIKM '08*, pages 1301–1310, New York, NY, USA. ACM.

Kai-Hsiang Yang, Shui-Shi Chen, Ming-Tai Hsieh, Hahn-Ming Lee, and Jan-Ming Ho. 2008. CRE: An automatic citation record extractor for publication list pages. In *Proc. WMWA'08 of PAKDD-2008*, Osaka, Japan, May.

Yanhong Zhai and Bing Liu. 2005. Web data extraction based on partial tree alignment. In *Proc. WWW '05*, pages 76–85, New York, NY, USA. ACM.

Jun Zhu, Zaiqing Nie, Ji-Rong Wen, Bo Zhang, and Wei-Ying Ma. 2006. Simultaneous record detection and attribute labeling in web data extraction. In *Proc. KDD '06*, pages 494–503, New York, NY, USA. ACM.

Citations in the Digital Library of Classics: Extracting Canonical References by Using Conditional Random Fields

Matteo Romanello, Federico Boschetti, Gregory Crane
The Perseus Project
Medford, MA, USA
matteo.romanello, federico.boschetti, gregory.crane{@tufts.edu}

Abstract

Scholars of Classics cite ancient texts by using abridged citations called canonical references. In the scholarly digital library, canonical references create a complex textile of links between ancient and modern sources reflecting the deep hypertextual nature of texts in this field. This paper aims to demonstrate the suitability of Conditional Random Fields (CRF) for extracting this particular kind of reference from unstructured texts in order to enhance the capabilities of navigating and aggregating scholarly electronic resources. In particular, we developed a parser which recognizes word level n-grams of a text as being canonical references by using a CRF model trained with both positive and negative examples.

1 Introduction

In the field of Classics, canonical references are the traditional way established by scholars to cite primary sources within secondary sources. By primary sources we mean essentially the ancient texts that are the specific research object of Philology, whereas by secondary sources we indicate all the modern publications containing scholarly interpretations about those ancient texts. This specific characteristic strongly differentiates canonical references from the typical references we usually find within research papers.

Canonical references are used to shortly refer to the research object itself (in this case ancient texts) rather than to the existing literature about a certain topic, as happens with references to other secondary sources. Given this distinction, canonical references assume a role of primary importance as the main entry point to the information contained in scholarly digital libraries of Classics. To find a parallel with other research fields, the role played by those references is somewhat analogous with that played by protein names in the medical literature or by notations of chemical compounds in the field of Chemistry. As was recently shown by Doms and Schroeder (2005) protein names can be used to semantically index documents and thus to enhance the information retrieval from a digital library of texts, provided that they are properly organized by using an ontology or a controlled vocabulary. Moreover, by analyzing and indexing such references as if they were backlinks (Lester, 2007) from a secondary to a primary source, it is possible to provide quantitative data about the impact of an ancient author for research in a particular disciplinary field, or in relation to a limited corpus of texts (e.g., the papers published by scholarly journals in a given time interval).

In addition to serving as entry points to information, canonical references can also be thought of as a navigation apparatus that allows scholars to browse seamlessly through ancient texts and modern interpretations about them (Crane, 1987). For every scholar working on the ancient historiographer Herodotus, for instance, it would be extremely useful to be able to easily access all the secondary sources containing references to Herodotus' works.

Therefore, the ability to automatically identify canonical references within unstructured texts is a first and necessary step to provide the users of digital libraries of Classics with a more sophisticated way to access information and to navigate through the texts that are already available to scholars of other fields.

The volume of publicly available digitized books constituting what has been called the Million Book Library (Crane, 2006) has made it essential to develop automatic and scalable tools to automate the process of information extraction from electronic resources. Furthermore, the obso-

Proceedings of the 2009 Workshop on Text and Citation Analysis for Scholarly Digital Libraries, ACL-IJCNLP 2009, pages 80–87,
Suntec, Singapore, 7 August 2009.

lescence time for publications is far longer in Classics than in other disciplines, meaning that typically the value of a publication does not decrease drastically after a certain time. As a result, scholars in Classics may be the most potential beneficiaries of the recent mass digitization initiatives, since they have already started with many materials out of copyright.

In this paper we describe how Conditional Random Fields (Lafferty et al., 2001), the state of the art model in automatic classification, can be suitably applied to provide a scalable solution to this problem.

2 Related work

Canonical references to primary sources can be explored from at least three different angles: 1) identification and extraction; 2) hypertextual navigation; 3) semantics.

The identification and extraction of bibliographic references from what we called secondary sources (i.e. monographs, commentaries, journal papers, etc.) is a well explored task for which effective tools already exist. Although the biggest efforts in this direction have been made in the scientific fields, those tools can also be suitably adapted to the field of Classics, since they are essentially based on machine learning techniques.

Several researchers recently focused on applying computational linguistics methods to automatically extract information from both Classical texts and modern texts about them, in order to support the above described needs of scalability. Gerlach and Crane (2008), and Kolak and Schilit (2008) considered the identification of citations within primary sources by analyzing the syntactic and morphological features of texts, while (Smith and Crane, 2001) dealt with the disambiguation of geographical names.

Looking at the problem of canonical references from the user point of view, a digital library of Classical texts such as the Perseus Digital Library[1]. already offers to the reader the ability to navigate from secondary sources to the primary sources they refer to, a process called reference linking. The identification of references and the attribution of semantics to them, however, was done manually, and the navigation is limited to resources contained in the same text collection. An analogous reference linking system was proposed by Romanello (2008) as a value added service that could be provided to readers of electronic journals by leveraging semantic encoded canonical references.

(Smith, 2009) provided an essential contribution to the research concerning the semantics of canonical references. The Canonical Text Services (CTS) protocol[2] was developed by Smith for Harvard's Center for Hellenic Studies; it is based on URNs and is aimed at providing a machine actionable equivalent to printed canonical references. This protocol allows us to translate those references into machine actionable URNs that can then be resolved through resolution services against a distributed digital library of texts. The innovative aspect of the CTS protocol consists of a loose coupling system by which the linking between primary and secondary sources can be realized. Instead of hard linking a canonical reference to just one electronic edition of a primary source, by embedding the CTS URNs inside (X)HTML pages, it becomes possible to link it to an open ended number of resources as shown by (Romanello, 2007).

3 Canonical Text References

Canonical references present unique characteristics when compared to bibliographic references to modern publications. First of all, they do not refer to physical facts of the referred work (such as publication date or page number), but refer rather to its logical and hierarchical structure. In addition, canonical references often provide additional information needed by the reader to resolve the reference. For example "Archestr. fr. 30.1 Olson-Sens" means line 1 of fragment 30 of the comic poet Archestratus in the edition published by S. D. Olson and A. Sens in 1994.

The specification of the edition according to which a source is cited is an important piece of information to be considered. Indeed, since the aim of Philology is to reconstruct for ancient works a text that is as close as possible to the original one (given that the original text may have been corrupted over centuries of manuscript tradition), editors and scholars often disagree substantially as to what readings and conjectures have to be included in the established text.

Although some well established sets of abbreviations exist, scholars' practice of citing primary

[1] `http://www.perseus.tufts.edu/hopper/`

[2] `http://chs75.harvard.edu/projects/diginc/techpub/cts`

sources may noticeably differ according to style preferences and the typographical needs of publishers, journals or research groups. Aeschylus' name might appear in the abridged forms "A., Aesch., Aeschyl.", and similarly a collection of fragments like Jacoby's *Die Fragmente der Grieschischen Historiker* may be abbreviated either as FrGrHist or FGrHist.

Moreover, some highly specialized branches of research exist within the field of Classics, such as those dedicated to Epic poetry or Tragedy, or even to a single author like Aeschylus or Homer. In those specialized branches a common tendency to use shorter references with a higher semantic density for the most cited authors can be observed. For example, in publications containing thousands of references to Homer's *Iliad* and *Odyssey*, references to these texts are often expressed with Greek letters indicating the book number along with the verse number (e.g., "α 1" stands for the first verse of the first book of Homer's *Odyssey*). Lowercase letters are used to refer to books of the *Odyssey*, whereas uppercase letters refer to the books of the *Iliad*, according to a practice developed in the IV century B.C. by scholars of the library at Alexandria.

In the actual practice of scholarly writing, canonical references can appear with slightly different figures according to the needs of narrative. Along with complete canonical references to a single text passage, expressed as either a single value or a range of values, other references can often be found that are missing one or more components that are normally present within canonical references, such as an indication of the author name, of the work title or of the editor name (e.g., "Hom. Od. 9.1, 9.2-3; Il 1.100"). This happens particularly in subsequent references to passages of the same work.

Those differences that can be observed about the appearance of canonical references require us to apply different processing strategies to each case. We focus on the task of automatically identifying complete references to primary sources. Once those references have been identified in the input document, we can find other anaphoric references by applying some scope-based parsing. Indeed, a canonical reference in the text constitutes the *reference scope* for subsequent text passage indications referring to the same work.

4 Methodology

Provided that scholars may use canonical references with different abbreviation or citation styles, it is nevertheless possible to identify within canonical references common patterns in terms of token features.

CRF is used to classify a token depending on its features and is suitable to identify those feature patterns (Culotta et al., 2006). During the training phase, the CRF model learns what features make it more likely for a token to belong to a given category.

Our starting assumption is that it is possible to determine if a sequence of tokens constitute a canonical reference by evaluating (looking at) the features of its tokens. Each token of a sequence is assigned a category on the basis of a fixed number of features. Those token categories are in turn used as features to classify the token sequence.

Starting from a dataset of canonical references and applying the above described criteria to assign features to the tokens, we obtain a training dataset where each canonical reference is reduced to a token by removing whitespaces, and it is a assigned as many as features as the category assigned to its tokens.

Finally, in order to classify token sequences as "references" or "non-references" each canonical reference is assigned a convenient label. The obtained set of labelled references is used to train a CRF model to identify canonical references within unstructured texts.

4.1 Feature Extraction and Token Categorization

For feature extraction phase, it was important to identify both inclusive and exclusive token features. Indeed, to extract canonical references with a high level of precision, we need to identify not only the characteristic features of tokens occurring within actual references but also those characteristic features for tokens occurring in sequences that we want to be classified as non-references.

Even though the features are quite similar to those used to identify modern bibliographic references (Isaac Councill and Kan, 2008), they were tuned to fit the specific needs of canonical references to primary sources. We decided to record a total of 9 features for each token, concerning the following aspects:

1. *Punctuation*: information about the punctuation concerning the presence of a final dot, hyphen, quotation marks and brackets (either single or paired), and marks used to divide and structure sequences (i.e. comma, colon and semicolon), which are particularly important for sequences of text passages.

2. *Orthographic Case*: the orthographic case of a token is an essential piece of information to be tracked. Author names when abbreviated still keep the initial as an uppercase letter, whereas collections of texts (such as collections of fragments) often present all uppercase or mixed case letters (e.g., "TrGrFr","CGF", "FHG", etc.).

3. *Stopwords*: given that the main language of the input document is passed as a parameter to the parser, we record in a separate feature information regarding whether a token is a stopword in the input document language. This feature is particularly important in determining more precisely the actual boundaries of a canonical reference within the text.

4. *Greek Words*: since we deal with Unicode UTF-8 text, we distinguish Greek letters and words. This allows us to identify more precisely those references that contain Greek text such as the above mentioned Homeric references or references to the ancient lexica (e.g., Harpocr., Lex. s.v. Παναθήναια) since they contain the lemma of the Greek word referred to, usually preceded by the abbreviation "s.v." (i.e. sub voce).

5. *Number*: Roman and Arabic numerals combined in several figures are frequently used to indicate the scope of a reference. Arabic numerals that are used to represent modern dates, however, are distinguished by using a heuristic (for example, consider the problem of a footnote mark which gets appended to a date). Nevertheless, sequences of both numbers and punctuation marks are assigned a specific value for this feature, since the scope of a reference is commonly expressed by dot and hyphen separated sequences such as "9.235-255".

6. *Dictionary matching*: two features are assigned if a token matches a dictionary entry. Three different dictionaries are used to verify if a token corresponds to a known canonical abbreviation (e.g. "Hom." for Homer or "Od." for *Odyssey*) or to another kind of abbreviation, namely the abbreviations used by philologists to shortly refer to pages, lines, verses, etc. ("p", "pp.", "v.", "vv.", "cfr", etc.) or to abbreviations used for modern journals. Abbreviations pertaining to the latter kind are likely to introduce some noise during the n-gram classification phase and thus are properly distinguished through a specific feature. During preliminary analysis we particularly observed that journal abbreviations were often confused with abbreviations for text collections since - as we noted above - they share the feature of having uppercase or mixed case letters.

7. *Fragment indication*: canonical references to fragments usually contain the indication "fr." (and "frr." for more than one). Therefore we expect tokens bearing this feature to occur almost exclusively within references to fragmentary texts.

We extract from the training dataset those unique patterns of these 9 token features that are likely to be found within canonical references. In order to ensure both the scalability and the extensibility of the suggested method to disciplinary fields other than Classics, we did not assign an identity feature to tokens or - in other words - the actual string content is not considered as a token feature. However, since this decision might decrease the overall precision of the system, we introduced some features to record whether the token string occurs in one or more controlled dictionaries (e.g., list of widely adopted abbreviations).

An analogous consideration is valid also for the dependency of the system from a specific language. Even though the approach is substantially language independent, the performances of our system in terms of precision were improved by using language specific lists of stopwords in order to identify the actual boundaries of a canonical reference within the text. Currently we support the most commonly used languages in the field of Classics (English, French, German, Italian, Spanish).

Finally, it is worth noting that the use of italics is a distinctive feature in particular for those tokens that represent abbreviations of work titles. Since we are dealing with plain text input documents, however, and wish to keep the adopted approach as generalizable as possible, this feature has not been taken into account.

Token	Features									Cat.
	F1	F2	F3	F4	F5	F6	F7	F8	F9	
Od.	ICP	FDT	NOD	OTH	OTH	OTH	CAB	OTH	OTH	1_c50
9.216-535.	OTH	FDT	DSN	OTH	OTH	OTH	OTH	OTH	OTH	2_c6

Table 1: Categorization of tokens of the reference "Od. 9.216-535" on the basis of their features.

Token	Features		Cat.
	F1	F2	
Od._9.216-535	1_c50	2_c6	ref

Table 2: Categorization of the reference of Tab. 1 by using token categories as its features.

Feature Label	
F1	Case
F2	Punctuation Mark
F3	Number
F4	Greek Sequence
F5	Stop Word
F6	Paired Brackets
F7	Contained in the 1st Dict.
F8	Contained in the 2nd Dict.
F9	Fragment Indication
Feature Value	
CAB	Canonical Abbreviation
DSN	Dot Separated Number Plus Range
FDT	Final Dot
ICP	Initial Cap
NOD	No Digit Sequence
OTH	Other

Table 3: List of abbreviations used in Tab. 1, 2.

4.2 Positive and Negative Training

Since the main goal of our parser is to identify canonical references by isolating them from the surrounding context, both positive and negative training examples are needed. Indeed, provided two token sequences where the first contains just a canonical reference (e.g., "Od. 9.216-535") and the second additionally includes some tokens from the context phrase (e.g.,"Od. 9.216-535, cfr. p. 29."), without a negative training phrase both token sequences would have the same degree of similarity. When weighted by the CRF model the result would be that both sequences would share the same number of features with one of the references of the positive training. But since other sequences presenting features from both the positive and negative training were included in the training, and since such sequences were labelled as "non-references", the end result is that a token sequence with some tokens from a context phrase will be less similar to a pure canonical reference.

The first step of the training phase is the extraction of token features and the identification of unique patterns of token features. At this stage the processing units are the tokens of a reference. Given a dataset of canonical references, each reference is firstly tokenized and each token is then assigned 9 labels containing the values for the above described features (see Section 4.1). Note that in Tab. 1, 2 the labels and values of features are indicated by the abbreviations given in Tab. 3.

The observed combinations of feature values are then deduplicated and rearranged into unique categories that are used to classify each token (see Tab 1). These categories correspond to the uniques combinations of features assigned to tokens of references in the training dataset. Each category is defined by a name such as "c6" or "c50", where "c" simply stands for 'category'" and "6" or "50" are unique numeric identifiers. Besides, a numerical prefix corresponding to the position of the token inside the canonical reference is then added to the category name to form the identifier. Indeed, the position of each token in the sequence is in itself meaningful information, provided that indications of the reference scope (and other reference components as well) tend to occur at the end of the token sequence. What we obtain are category identifiers such as "1_c50" or "2_c6".

The second step is building the training dataset. At this stage each canonical reference is reduced to a single token which is assigned the label "ref" (i.e. reference) and which has as distinctive features the category identifiers assigned to its tokens (see Tab 2).

Finally, a such obtained dataset of labelled instances is used to train our CRF model by using the Java CRF implementation provided by the Mallet toolkit (McCallum, 2002).

4.3 Sequence Classification Process

The system we propose to identify canonical references in unstructured texts is basically a binary classifier. Indeed, it classifies as "reference" or "non-reference" a sequence of word level n-grams depending on the features of its tokens. However, in the training dataset the positive examples are manually grouped by typology and different labels (such as "ref1", "ref2" etc.) are assigned to canonical references pertaining to different types. This is done in order to avoid associating too many features to a single class and thus to maximize the difference in terms of features between sequence being references and non-references.

Since every token is assigned a certain number of features and finally a category, the likelihood for a token sequence to be a canonical reference can be determined on the basis of its similarity, in terms of token features, to the labelled references of a training set.

Once the input document is tokenized into single words, the n-grams are created by using a window of variable dimensions ranging from the minimum to the maximum length in terms of tokens that was observed for all the references in the training dataset. For example, provided that the shortest canonical reference in the training dataset is 2 tokens long and the longest is 7 tokens long, for each token are created 6 word level n-grams.

For the sake of performance, however, the number of n-grams to be created is determined for each token at parsing time. First of all a threshold value is passed to the parser as an option value. The threshold is compared to the weight value assigned by the CRF model to the probability of a token to be classified with a label, in our case "ref" or "noref". For each token, if the first n-gram is classified as not being a canonical reference the processing shifts to the next token, since we observed that if the first n-gram is classified as a non-reference the following n-grams of increasing width never contain a reference. If the examined n-gram is classified as reference, another of dimension n+1 is created: the parser passes on to process the next token only if the current n-gram is classified as a canonical reference with a likelihood value greater that that of the previous n-gram.

5 Training and Evaluation Criteria

The system is based on both a positive and a negative training.

The dataset for the positive training is built by labeling with the above explained criteria a starting set of approximatively 50 canonical references selected by an expert. The classifier trained with those positive examples is then applied to a random set of documents. Extracted candidate canonical references are scored by the CRF model by assigning to each sequence of n-grams a value representing the probability for the sequence to be a canonical reference.

The first one hundred errors with the highest score, due to the sharing of several features with the actual canonical references, are marked as non-references and added to the set of sequences to use for the negative training. The negative training is needed in order to precisely segment a canonical reference and to correctly classify those sequences that are most likely to be confused with actual canonical references, such as sequences only partially containing a canonical reference or bibliographic references. In particular, bibliographic references are misleading sequences since they have several features in common with canonical references, such as capitalized titles and page numbers.

The overall performances of the system on a random sample of 24 pages can be summarized by: precision=81.01%, recall=94.11%, accuracy=77.11%, F-score=0.8707. Analytical data are provided in Tab. 4. Although the evaluation was performed on pages drawn from a publication written in Italian, we expect to have analogous performances on texts written in each of the currently supported languages (English, French, German, Italian, Spanish) for the reasons described in Section 4.1.

The results are encouraging, however, and some further improvements could concern the recovery of tokens wrongly included in or excluded from the sequence identified by the parser.

6 Conclusion and Future Work

This paper has illustrated how the CRF model can be suitably applied to the task of extracting canonical references from unstructured texts by correctly classifying word level n-grams as references or non-references.

Document #	Precision	Recall	Accuracy	F-Score
40	100.00%	100.00%	100.00%	1.0000
41	100.00%	100.00%	100.00%	1.0000
55	100.00%	100.00%	100.00%	1.0000
57	100.00%	100.00%	100.00%	1.0000
62	100.00%	100.00%	100.00%	1.0000
64	100.00%	100.00%	100.00%	1.0000
67	25.00%	25.00%	25.00%	0.2500
74	88.00%	87.50%	77.78%	0.8800
77	45.00%	90.00%	42.86%	0.6000
82	100.00%	100.00%	100.00%	1.0000
85	100.00%	90.00%	90.00%	0.9474
88	100.00%	100.00%	100.00%	1.0000
90	92.31%	92.31%	85.71%	0.4286
100	100.00%	100.00%	100.00%	1.0000
113	60.00%	100.00%	60.00%	0.7500
117	100.00%	100.00%	100.00%	1.0000
134	100.00%	75.00%	75.00%	0.8571
137	75.00%	100.00%	75.00%	0.8571
144	67.00%	100.00%	67.00%	0.8024
146	33.00%	100.00%	33.00%	0.4511
150	57.14%	100.00%	57.00%	0.7273
162	100.00%	100.00%	100.00%	1.0000
169	50.00%	75.00%	43.00%	0.6000
Overall	81.01%	94.11%	77.11%	0.8707

Table 4: Performance evaluation of the system.

Once automatically identified, canonical references can have further semantic information added to them. By combining and then applying techniques of syntactic and semantic parsing to the identified references, it is possible to extract information such as the precise author name and work title, the text passage referred to, and the reference edition (either when implicitly assumed or explicitly declared).

The first important outcome of our work is that such an automatic system allows us to elicit the hidden tangle of references which links together the primary and secondary sources of a digital library. Another important outcome is that unstructured texts could be analyzed on the basis of the canonical references they contain, for example by clustering techniques. Given a consistent corpus of texts it would be possible to cluster it on the basis of the distribution of canonical references within documents in order to obtain a first topic classification.

Among the benefits of the proposed approach there is the possibility of applying it to texts pertaining to specific branches of Classics, like Papyrology or Epigraphy. Indeed in those disciplines papyri and epigraphs are also often cited by abridged references that are very similar in their structure and features to the canonical text references. In a similar way, a canonical reference parser can be trained on a particular citation style in order to tailor it to a consistent corpus of texts with consequent improvements on the overall performances.

Finally, since the task of automatic extraction of canonical references has never been explored before, we hope that in the future more resources will be available for this task (such as training datasets, golden standards, performance measure to be compared, etc.), analogous to those already existing for other more common tasks, like named entity recognition or the extraction and labeling of modern bibliographic references.

References

Gregory Crane. 1987. From the old to the new: intergrating hypertext into traditional scholarship. In *Proceedings of the ACM conference on Hypertext*, pages 51–55, Chapel Hill, North Carolina, United States. ACM.

Gregory Crane. 2006. What do you do with a million books. *D-Lib Magazine*, 12(3).

Aron Culotta, Andrew Mccallum, and Jonathan Betz. 2006. Integrating probabilistic extraction models and data mining to discover relations and patterns in text. In *Proceedings of the main conference on Human Language Technology Conference of the North American Chapter of the Association of Computational Linguistics*, pages 296–303, Morristown, NJ, USA. Association for Computational Linguistics.

Andreas Doms and Michael Schroeder. 2005. GoPubMed: exploring PubMed with the gene ontology. *Nucl. Acids Res.*, 33(suppl_2):783–786, July.

Andrea Ernst-Gerlach and Gregory Crane, 2008. *Identifying Quotations in Reference Works and Primary Materials*, pages 78–87.

C. Lee Giles Isaac Councill and Min-Yen Kan. 2008. Parscit: an open-source crf reference string parsing package. In Bente Maegaard Joseph Mariani Jan Odjik Stelios Piperidis Daniel Tapias Nicoletta Calzolari (Conference Chair), Khalid Choukri, editor, *Proceedings of the Sixth International Language Resources and Evaluation (LREC'08)*, Marrakech, Morocco. European Language Resources Association (ELRA). http://www.lrec-conf.org/proceedings/lrec2008/.

Okan Kolak and Bill N. Schilit. 2008. Generating links by mining quotations. In *Proceedings of the nineteenth ACM conference on Hypertext and hypermedia*, pages 117–126, Pittsburgh, PA, USA. ACM.

John Lafferty, Andrew Mccallum, and Fernando Pereira. 2001. Conditional random fields: Probabilistic models for segmenting and labeling sequence data. In *Proc. 18th International Conf. on Machine Learning*, pages 289, 282. Morgan Kaufmann, San Francisco, CA.

Frank Lester. 2007. Backlinks: Alternatives to the citation index for determining impact. *Journal of Electronic Publishing*, 10(2).

Andrew Kachites McCallum. 2002. MALLET: a machine learning for language toolkit. http://mallet.cs.umass.edu.

Matteo Romanello. 2007. A semantic linking system for canonical references to electronic corpora. Prague. to be next published in the proceedings of the ECAL 2007 Electronic Corpora of Ancient Languages, held in Prague November 2007.

Matteo Romanello. 2008. A semantic linking framework to provide critical value-added services for e-journals on classics. In Susanna Mornati and Leslie Chan, editors, *ELPUB2008. Open Scholarship: Authority, Community, and Sustainability in the Age of Web 2.0 - Proceedings of the 12th International Conference on Electronic Publishing held in Toronto, Canada 25-27 June 2008 / Edited by: Leslie Chan and Susanna Mornati.*

David A. Smith and Gregory Crane. 2001. Disambiguating geographic names in a historical digital library. In *ECDL '01: Proceedings of the 5th European Conference on Research and Advanced Technology for Digital Libraries*, pages 127–136, London, UK. Springer-Verlag.

Neel Smith. 2009. Citation in classical studies. *Digital Humanities Quarterly*, 3(1).

Automatic Extraction of Citation Contexts for Research Paper Summarization: A Coreference-chain based Approach

Dain Kaplan **Ryu Iida** **Takenobu Tokunaga**
Department of Computer Science
Tokyo Institute of Technology
{dain,ryu-i,take}@cl.cs.titech.ac.jp

Abstract

This paper proposes a new method based on coreference-chains for extracting citations from research papers. To evaluate our method we created a corpus of citations comprised of citing papers for 4 cited papers. We analyze some phenomena of citations that are present in our corpus, and then evaluate our method against a cue-phrase-based technique. Our method demonstrates higher precision by 7–10%.

1 Introduction

Review and comprehension of existing research is fundamental to the ongoing process of conducting research; however, the ever increasing volume of research papers makes accomplishing this task increasingly more difficult. To mitigate this problem of information overload, a form of knowledge reduction may be necessary.

Past research (Garfield et al., 1964; Small, 1973) has shown that citations contain a plethora of latent information available and that much can be gained by exploiting it. Indeed, there is a wealth of literature on topic-clustering, e.g. bibliographic coupling (Kessler, 1963), or co-citation analysis (Small, 1973). Subsequent research demonstrated that citations could be clustered on their quality, using keywords that appeared in the running-text of the citation (Weinstock, 1971; Nanba et al., 2000; Nanba et al., 2004; Teufel et al., 2006).

Similarly, other work has shown the utility in the IR domain of ranking the relevance of cited papers by using supplementary index terms extracted from the content of citations in citing papers, including methods that search through a fixed character-length window (O'Connor, 1982; Bradshaw, 2003), or that focus solely on the sentence containing the citation (Ritchie et al., 2008) for acquiring these terms. A prior case study (Ritchie et al., 2006) pointed out the challenges in proper identification of the full span of a citation in running text and acknowledged that fixed-width windows have their limits. In contrast to this, endeavors have been made to extract the entire span of a citation by using cue-phrases collected and deemed salient by statistical merit (Nanba et al., 2000; Nanba et al., 2004). This has met in evaluations with some success.

The Cite-Sum system (Kaplan and Tokunaga, 2008) also aims at knowledge reduction through use of citations. It receives a paper title as a query and attempts to generate a summary of the paper by finding citing papers[1] and extracting citations in the running-text that refer to the paper. Before outputting a summary, it also classifies extracted citation text, and removes citations with redundant content. Another similar study (Qazvinian and Radev, 2008) aims at using the content of citations within citing papers to generate summaries of fields of research.

It is clear that merit exists behind extraction of citations in running text. This paper proposes a new method for performing this task based on coreference-chains. To evaluate our method we created a corpus of citations comprised of citing papers for 4 cited papers. We also analyze some phenomena of citations that are present in our corpus.

The paper organization is as follows. We first define terminology, discuss the construction of our corpus and the results found through its analysis, and then move on to our proposed method using coreference-chains. We evaluate the proposed method by using the constructed corpus, and then conclude the paper.

[1] Papers are downloaded automatically from the web.

Proceedings of the 2009 Workshop on Text and Citation Analysis for Scholarly Digital Libraries, ACL-IJCNLP 2009, pages 88–95,
Suntec, Singapore, 7 August 2009.

2 Terminology

So that we may dispense with convoluted explanations for the rest of this paper, we introduce several terms.

An *anchor* is the string of characters that marks the occurrence of a citation in the running-text of a paper, such as "(Fakeman 2007)" or "[57]".[2] The sentence that this anchor resides within is then the *anchor sentence*. The citation continues from before and after this anchor as long as the text continues to refer to the cited work; this block of text may span more than a single sentence. We introduce the *citation-site*, or *c-site* for short, to represent this block of text that discusses the cited work. Since more than once sentence may discuss the cited work, each of these sentences is called a *c-site sentence*. For clarity will also call the anchor the *c-site anchor* henceforth. A *citing paper* contains the c-site that refers to the *cited paper*. Finally, the *reference* at the end of the paper provides details about a c-site anchor (and the c-site).

Figure 1 shows a sample c-site with the c-site anchor wavy-underlined, and the c-site itself italicized; the non-italicized text is unrelated to the c-site. The reference for this c-site is also provided below the dotted line. In all subsequent examples, the c-site will be in italics and the current place of emphasis wavy-underlined.

> "...Our area of interest is plant growth. *In past research* (Fakeman et al., 2001), *the relationship between sunlight and plant growth was shown to directly correlate. It was also shown to adhere to simple equations for deducing this relationship, the equation varying by plant.* We propose a method that ..."
>
> ....
>
> J. Fakeman: Changing Plant Growth Factors during Global Warming. In: *Proceedings of SCANLP 2001.*

Figure 1: A sample c-site and its reference

3 Corpus Construction and Analysis

We created a corpus comprised of 38 papers citing 4 (cited) papers taken from *Computational Linguistics: Special Issue on the Web as Corpus*, Volume 29, Number 3, 2003 as our data set and preprocessed it to automatically mark c-site anchors to facilitate the annotation process. The citing papers were downloaded from CiteSeer-X;[3] see Table 1 for details.

We then proceeded to manually annotate the corpus using SLAT (Noguchi et al., 2008), a browser-based multi-purpose annotation tool. We devised the following guidelines for annotation. Since the tool allows for two types of annotation, namely *segments* that demarcate a region of text, and *links*, that allow an annotator to assign relationships between them, we created four segment types and three link types. Segments were used to mark c-site anchors, c-sites, background information (explained presently), and references. We used the term *background information* to refer to any running-text that elaborates on a c-site but is not strictly part of the c-site itself (refer to Figure 2 for an example). Even during annotation, however, we encountered situations that felt ambiguous, making this a rather contentious issue.

Our corpus had a limited number of background information annotations, or we would likely have experienced more issues. That being said, it is at least important to recognize that such kinds of supplementary content exist (that may not be part of the c-site but is still beneficial to be included), and needs to be considered more in the future.

We then linked each c-site to its anchor, each anchor to its reference, and any background information to the c-site supplemented. We also decided on annotating entire sentences, even if only part of a sentence referred to the cited paper. Table 1 outlines our corpus.

Table 1: Corpus composition

Paper ID	1	2	3	4	Total
Citing papers	2	14	15	7	38
C-sites	3	17	18	12	50
C-site sentences	6	27	33	28	94

To our knowledge, this is the first corpus constructed in the context of paper summarization related to collections of citing papers.[4]

Analysis of the corpus provided some interesting insights, though a larger corpus is required to confirm the frequency and validity of such phenomena. The more salient discoveries are itemized below. These phenomena may also co-occur.

[2] In practice the anchor does not include brackets, though the brackets do signal the start/end of the anchor. This is because multiple anchors may be present at once, e.g. (Fakeman 2007; Noman 2008).

[3] `http://citeseerx.ist.psu.edu`

[4] Though not specific to the task of summarization through use of c-sites, citation corpora have been constructed in the past, e.g. (Teufel et al., 2006).

Background Information Though not strictly part of a c-site, background information may need to be included for the citation to be comprehensible. Take Figure 2 for example (background information is wavy-underlined) for the c-site anchor "(Resnik & Smith 2003)". The authors insert their own research into the c-site (illustrated with wavy-underlines); this information is important for understanding the following c-site sentence, but is not strictly discussing the cited paper. Background information is thus a form of "meta-information" about the c-site.

In well written papers, often the flow of content is gradual, which can make distinguishing background information difficult.

> "...*Resnik and his colleagues (Resnik & Smith 2003) proposed a new approach, STRAND, ...The databases for parallel texts in several languages with download tools are available from the STRAND webpage. Recently they also applied the same technique for collecting a set of links to monolingual pages identified as Russian by http://www.archive.org, and Internet archiving service.* We have evaluated the Russian database produced by this method and identified a number of serious problems with it. *First, it does not identify the time when the page was downloaded and stored in the Internet archive* ..."

Figure 2: A non-contiguous c-site w/ background information (from (Sharoff, 2006))

Contiguity C-sites are not necessarily contiguous. We found in fact that authors tend to insert opinions or comments related to their own work with sentences/clauses in between actual c-site sentences/clauses, that would be best omitted from the c-site. In Figure 2 the wavy-underlined text shows the author's opinion portion. This creates problems for cue-phrase based techniques, as though they detect the sentence *following* it, they fail on the opinion sentence. Incorporation of a leniency for a gap in such techniques may be possible, but seems more problematic and likely to misidentify c-site sentences altogether.

Related/Itemization Authors often list several works (namely, insert several c-site anchors) in the same sentence using connectives. The works may likely be related, and though this may be useful information for certain tasks, it is important to differentiate which material is related to the c-site, and which is the c-site itself.

In Figure 3 the second sentence discusses both c-site anchors (and should be included in both their c-sites); the first sentence, however, contains two main clauses connected with a connective, each clause a different c-site (one with the anchor "[3]" and one with "[4]"). Sub-clausal analysis is necessary for resolving issues such as these. For our current task, however, we annotated only sentences, and so in this example the second c-site anchor is included in the first.

> "... *STRAND system [4] searches the web for parallel text* and [3] extracts translations pairs among anchor texts pointing together to the same webpage. *However they all suffered from the lack of such bilingual resources available on the web* ..."

Figure 3: Itemized c-sites partially overlapping (from (Zhang et al., 2005))

Nesting C-sites may be nested. In Figure 4 the nested citation ("[Lafferty and Zhai 2001, Lavrenko and Croft 2001]") *should* be included in the parent one ("[Kraaij et al. 2002]"). The wavy-underlined portion shows the sentence needed for full comprehension of the c-site.

> "... *In recent years, the use of language models in IR has been a great success [Lafferty and Zhai 2001, Lavrenko and Croft 2001]. It is possible to extend the approach to CLIR by integrating a translation model. This is the approach proposed in [Kraaij et al. 2002]* ..."

Figure 4: Separate c-site anchors does not mean separate c-sites (from (Nie, 2002))

Aliases Figure 5 demonstrates another issue: aliasing. The author redefines how they cite the paper, in this case using the acronym "K&L".

> "... *To address the data-sparsity issue, we employed the technique used in Keller and Lapata (2003, K&L) to get a more robust approximation of predicate-argument counts. K&L use this technique to obtain frequencies for predicate-argument bigrams that were unseen in a given corpus, showing that the massive size of the web outweighs the noisy and unbalanced nature of searches performed on it to produce statistics that correlate well with corpus data* ..."

Figure 5: C-Site with Aliasing for anchor "Keller and Lapata (2003, K&L)" (from (Kehler, 2004))

4 Coreference Chain-based Extraction

Some of the issues found in our corpus, namely identification of background information, non-contiguous c-sites, and aliases, show promise of

Table 2: Evaluation results for coreference resolution against the MUC-7 formal corpus.

	MUC-7 Task			Sentence Eval.		
System Setting	R	P	F	R	P	F
All Features	35.71	74.71	48.33	36.27	80.49	50.00
w/o SOON_STR_MATCH	48.35	83.81	61.32	48.35	88.00	62.41
w/o COSINE_SIMILARITY	46.70	82.52	59.65	46.70	86.73	60.71

resolution with coreference-chains. This is because coreference-chains match noun phrases that appear with other noun phrases to which they refer, a characteristic present in these three categories. On the other hand, cue-phrases do not detect any c-site sentence that does not use keywords (e.g. "In addition"). In the following section we discuss our implementation of a coreference chain-based extraction technique, and how we then applied it to the c-site extraction task. An analysis of the results then follows.

4.1 Training the Coreference Resolver

To create and train our coreference resolver, we used a combination of techniques as outlined originally by (Soon et al., 2001) and subsequently extended by (Ng and Cardie, 2002). Mimicking their approaches, we used the corpora provided for the MUC-7 coreference resolution task (LDC2001T02, 2001), which includes sets of newspaper articles, annotated with coreference relations, for both training and testing. They also outlined a list of features to extract for training the resolver to recognize the coreference relations. Specifically, (Soon et al., 2001) established a list of 12 features that compare a given anaphor with a candidate antecedent, e.g. gender agreement, number agreement, both being pronouns, both part of the same semantic class (i.e. WordNet synset hyponyms/hypernyms), etc.

For training the resolver, a corpus annotated with anaphors and their antecedents is processed, and pairs of anaphor and candidate antecedents are created so as to have only one positive instance per anaphor (the annotated antecedent). Negative examples are created by taking all occurrences of noun phrases that occur *between* the anaphor and its antecedent in the text. The antecedent in these steps is also always considered to be to the left of, or preceding, the anaphor; cataphors are not addressed in this technique.

We implemented, at least minimally, all 12 of these features, with a few additions of what (Ng and Cardie, 2002) hand selected as being most salient for increased performance. We also extended this list by adding a cosine-similarity metric between two noun phrases; it uses bag-of-words to create a vector for each noun phrase (where each word is a term in the vector) to compute their similarity. The intuition behind this is that noun phrases with more similar surface forms should be more likely to corefer.

We further optimized string recognition and plurality detection for handling citation-strings. See Table 3 for the full list of our features. While both (Soon et al., 2001) and (Ng and Cardie, 2002) induced decision trees (C5 and C4.5, respectively) we opted for using an SVM-based approach instead (Vapnik, 1998; Joachims, 1999). SVMs are known for being reliable and having good performance.

4.2 Evaluating the Coreference Resolver

We ran our trained SVM classifier against the MUC-7 formal evaluation corpus; the results are shown in Table 2.

The results using all features listed in Table 3 are inferior to those set forth by (Soon et al., 2001; Ng and Cardie, 2002); likely this is due to poorer selection of features. Upon analysis, it seems that half of the misidentified antecedents were still chosen within the correct sentence and more than 10% identified the proper antecedent, but selected the entire noun phrase (when that antecedent was marked as, for example, only its head); the majority of these cases involved the antecedent being only one sentence away from the anaphor. Since the former seemed suspect of a partial string matching feature, we decided to re-run the tests first excluding our implementation of the `SOON_STR_MATCH` feature, and then our `COSINE_SIMILARITY` feature. The results for this are shown in Table 2. It can be seen that using either of the two string comparison features works substantially better than with both of them in tandem, with the `COSINE_SIMILARITY` feature showing signs of overall better performance which is competitive to (Soon et al.,

Table 3: Features used for coreference resolution.

Feature	Possible Values	Brief Description (where necessary)
ANAPHOR_IS_PRONOUN	T/F	
ANAPHOR_IS_INDEFINITE	T/F	
ANAPHOR_IS_DEMONSTRATIVE	T/F	
ANTECEDENT_IS_PRONOUN	T/F	
ANTECEDENT_IS_EMBEDDED	T/F	Boolean indicating if the candidate antecedent is within another NP.
SOON_STR_MATCH	T/F	As per (Soon et al., 2001). Articles and demonstrative pronouns removed before comparing NPs. If any part of the NP matches between candidate and anaphor set to true (T); false otherwise.
ALIAS_MATCH	T/F	Creates abbreviations for organizations and proper names in an attempt to find an alias.
BOTH_PROPER_NAMES	T/F	
BOTH_PRONOUNS	T/F/–	
NUMBER_AGREEMENT	T/F/–	Basic morphological rules applied to the words to see if they are plural.
COSINE_SIMILARITY	NUM	A cosine similarity score between zero and one is applied to the head words of each NP.
GENDER_AGREEMENT	T/F/–	If the semantic class is Male or Female, use that gender, otherwise if a salutation is present, or lastly set to Unknown.
SEMANTIC_CLASS_AGREEMENT	T/F/–	Followed (Soon et al., 2001) specifications for using basic WordNet synsets, specifically: Female and Male belonging to Person, Organization, Location, Date, Time, Money, Percent belonging to Object. Any other semantic classes mapped to Unknown.

2001; Ng and Cardie, 2002). We exclude the SOON_STR_MATCH feature in the following experiments.

However, the MUC-7 task measures the ability to identity the proper antecedent from a list of candidates; the c-site extraction task is less ambitious in that it must only identify if a sentence contains the antecedent, not which noun phrase it is. When we evaluate our resolver using these loosened conditions it is expected that it will perform better.

To accomplish this we reevaluate the results from the resolver in a sentence-wise manner; we group the test instances by anaphor, and then by sentence. If any noun phrase within the sentence is marked as positive when there is in fact a positive noun phrase in the sentence, the sentence is marked as correct, and incorrect otherwise. The results in Table 2 for this simplified task show an increase in recall, and subsequently F-measure. The numbers for the loosened constraints evaluation are counted by sentence; the original is counted by noun phrase only.

Our system also generates many fewer training instances than the previous research, which we attribute to a more stringent noun phrase extraction procedure, but have not investigated thoroughly yet.

4.3 Application to the c-site extraction task

As outlined above, we used the resolver with the loosened constraints, namely evaluating the sentence a potential antecedent is in as likely or not, and not which noun phrase within the sentence is the actual antecedent. Using this principle as a base, we devised an algorithm for scanning sentences around a c-site anchor sentence to determine their likelihood of being part of the c-site. The algorithm, shown in simplified form in Figure 6, is described below.

Starting at the beginning of a c-site anchor sentence AS, scan left-to-right; for every noun phrase encountered within AS, begin a right-to-left sentence-by-sentence search; prepend any sentence S containing an antecedent above a certain likelihood THRESHOLD, until DISTANCE sentences have been scanned and no suitable candidate sentences have been found. We set the likelihood score to 1.0, tested ad-hoc for best results, and the distance-threshold to 5 sentences, having noted in our corpus that no citation is discontinuous by more than 4.

In a similar fashion, the algorithm then proceeds to scan text following AS; for every noun phrase NP encountered (moving left-to-right), begin a right-to-left search for a suitable antecedent. If a sentence is not evaluated above THRESHOLD,

Table 4: Evaluation results for c-site extraction w/o background information

	Sentence (Micro-average)			C-site (Macro-average)		
Method	R	P	F	R	P	F
Baseline 1 (anchor sentence)	53.2	100	69.4	74.6	100	85.5
Baseline 2 (random)	75.5	58.2	65.7	87.4	71.2	78.5
Cue-phrases (CP)	64.9	64.9	64.9	84.0	80.9	82.4
Coref-chains (CC))	64.9	74.4	69.3	81.0	87.2	84.0
CP/CC Union	74.5	58.8	65.7	88.4	75.0	81.1
CP/CC Intersection	55.3	91.2	69.0	76.6	95.7	85.1

```
set CSITE to AS

pre:
foreach NP in AS
  foreach sentence S preceding AS
    if DISTANCE > MAX-DIST goto post
    if likelihood > THRESHOLD then
      set CSITE to S + CSITE
      reset DISTANCE
    end
  end
end

post:
foreach sentence S after AS
  foreach NP in S
    foreach sentence S2 until S
      if DISTANCE > MAX-DIST stop
      if S2 has link then
        if likelihood > THRESHOLD then
          set S2 has link
        end
      end
    end
  end
end
```

Figure 6: Simplified c-site extraction algorithm using coreference-chains

it will be ignored when the algorithm backtracks to look for candidate noun phrases for a subsequent sentence, thus preserving the coreference-chain and preventing additional spurious chains. If more than `DISTANCE` sentences are scanned without finding a c-site sentence, the process is aborted and the collection of sentences returned.

4.4 Experiment Setup

To evaluate our coreference-chain extraction method we compare it with a cue-phrases technique (Nanba et al., 2004) and two baselines. Baseline 1 extracts only the c-site anchor sentence as the c-site; baseline 2 includes sentences before/after the c-site anchor sentence as part of the c-site with a 50/50 probability — it tosses a coin for each consecutive sentence to decide its inclusion. We also created two hybrid methods that combine the results of the cue-phrases and coreference-chain techniques, one the union of their results (includes the extracted sentences of both methods), and the other the intersection (includes sentences only for which both methods agree), to measure their mutual compatibility.

The annotated corpus provided the locations of c-site anchors for the cited paper within the citing paper's running-text. We then compared the extracted c-sites of each method to the c-sites of the annotated corpus.

4.5 Evaluation

The results of our experiments are presented in Table 4. We evaluated each method as follows. Recall and precision were measured for a c-site based on the number of extracted sentences; if an extracted sentence was annotated as part of the c-site, it counted as correct, and if an extracted sentence was not part of a c-site, incorrect; sentences annotated as being part of the c-site not extracted by the method counted as part of the total sentences for that c-site. As an example, if an annotated c-site has 3 sentences (including the c-site anchor sentence), and the evaluated method extracted 2 of these and 1 incorrect sentence, then the recall for this c-site using this method would be $2/3$, and the precision $2/(2+1)$.

Since the evaluation is inherently sentence-based, we provide two averages in Table 4. The micro-average is for sentences across all c-sites; in other words, we tallied the correct and incorrect sentence count for the whole corpus and then divided by the total number of sentences (94). This average provides a clearer picture on the efficacy of each method than does the macro-average. The macro-average was computed per c-site (as explained above) and then averaged over the total number of c-sites in the corpus (50).

With the exception of a 3% lead in macro-average recall, coreference-chains outperform cue-phrases in every way. We can see a substantial difference in micro-average precision (74.4 vs. 64.9), which results in nearly a 5% higher F-measure. The macro-average precision is also higher by more than 6%. It matches more and misses far less. The loss in the macro-average recall can be attributed to the coreference-chain method missing one of two sentences for several c-sites, which would lower its overall recall score; keep in mind that since in the macro-average all c-sites are treated equally, even large c-sites in which the coreference-chain method performs well, such an advantage will be reduced with averaging and is therefore misleading.

Baseline 2 performed as expected, i.e. higher than baseline 1 for recall. Looking only at F-measures for evaluating performance in this case is misleading. This is particularly the case because precision is more important than recall — we want accuracy. Coreference-chains achieved a precision of over 87.2 compared to the 71.2 of baseline 2.

The combined methods also showed promise. In particular, the intersection method had very high precision (91.2 and 95.7), and marginally managed to extract more sentences than baseline 1. The union method has more conservative scores.

We also understood from our corpus that only about half of c-sites were represented by c-site anchor sentences. The largest c-site in the corpus was 6 sentences, and the average 1.8. This means using the c-site anchor sentence alone excludes on average about half of the valuable data.

These results are promising, but a larger corpus is necessary to validate the results presented here.

5 Conclusions and Future Work

The results demonstrate that a coreference-chain-based approach may be useful to the c-site extraction task. We can also see that there is still much work to be done. The scores for the hybrid methods also indicate potential for a method that more tightly couples these two tasks, such as Rhetorical Structure Theory (RST) (Thompson and Mann, 1987; Marcu, 2000). Though it has demonstrated superior performance, coreference resolution is not a light-weight task; this makes real-time application more difficult than with cue-phrase-based approaches.

Our plans for future work include the construction of a larger corpus of c-sites, investigation of other features for improving our coreference resolver, and applying RST to c-site extraction.

Acknowledgments

The authors would like to express appreciation to Microsoft for their contribution to this research by selecting it as a recipient of the 2008 WEBSCALE Grant (Web-Scale NLP 2008, 2008).

References

Shannon Bradshaw. 2003. Reference directed indexing: Redeeming relevance for subject search in citation indexes. In *Proceedings of the 7th ECDL*, pages 499–510.

Eugene Garfield, Irving H. Sher, and Richard J. Torpie. 1964. *The use of citation data in writing the history of science*. Institute for Scientific Information, Philadelphia, Pennsylvania.

Thorsten Joachims. 1999. Making large-scale support vector machine learning practical. In Bernhard Schölkopf, Christopher J. C. Burges, and Alexander J. Smola, editors, *Advances in kernel methods: support vector learning*, pages 169–184. MIT Press, Cambridge, MA, USA.

Dain Kaplan and Takenobu Tokunaga. 2008. Sighting citation sites: A collective-intelligence approach for automatic summarization of research papers using c-sites. In *ASWC 2008 Workshops Proceedings*.

Andrew Kehler. 2004. The (non)utility of predicate-argument frequencies for pronoun interpretation. In *In: Proceedings of 2004 North American chapter of the Association for Computational Linguistics annual meeting*, pages 289–296.

M. M. Kessler. 1963. Bibliographic coupling between scientific papers. *American Documentation*, 14(1):10–25.

LDC2001T02. 2001. Message understanding conference (MUC) 7.

Daniel Marcu. 2000. The rhetorical parsing of unrestricted texts: A surface-based approach. *Computational Linguistics*, 26(3):395–448.

Hidetsugu Nanba, Noriko Kando, and Manabu Okumura. 2000. Classification of research papers using citation links and citation types: Towards automatic review article generation. In *Proceedings of 11th SIG/CR Workshop*, pages 117–134.

Hidetsugu Nanba, Takeshi Abekawa, Manabu Okumura, and Suguru Saito. 2004. Bilingual presri integration of multiple research paper databases. In *Proceedings of RIAO 2004*, pages 195–211, Avignon, France.

Vincent Ng and Claire Cardie. 2002. Improving machine learning approaches to coreference resolution. In *Proceedings of the 40th Annual Meeting on Association for Computational Linguistics*, pages 104–111.

J. Nie. 2002. Towards a unified approach to clir and multilingual ir. In *In: Workshop on Cross Language Information Retrieval: A Research Roadmap in the 25th Annual International ACM SIGIR Conference on Research and Development in Information Retrieval*, pages 8–14.

Masaki Noguchi, Kenta Miyoshi, Takenobu Tokunaga, Ryu Iida, Mamoru Komachi, and Kentaro Inui. 2008. Multiple purpose annotation using SLAT — Segment and link-based annotation tool —. In *Proceedings of 2nd Linguistic Annotation Workshop*, pages 61–64, May.

John O'Connor. 1982. Citing statements: Computer recognition and use to improve retrieval. *Information Processing & Management.*, 18(3):125–131.

Vahed Qazvinian and Dragomir R. Radev. 2008. Scientific paper summarization using citation summary networks.

Anna Ritchie, Simone Teufel, and Stephen Robertson. 2006. How to find better index terms through citations. In *Proceedings of the Workshop on How Can Computational Linguistics Improve Information Retrieval?*, pages 25–32, Sydney, Australia, July. Association for Computational Linguistics.

Anna Ritchie, Stephen Robertson, and Simone Teufel. 2008. Comparing citation contexts for information retrieval. In *CIKM '08: Proceedings of the 17th ACM conference on Information and knowledge management*, pages 213–222, New York, NY, USA. ACM.

Serge Sharoff. 2006. Creating general-purpose corpora using automated search engine queries. In *WaCky! Working papers on the Web as Corpus. Gedit.*

H. Small. 1973. Co-citation in the scientific literature: A new measure of the relationship between two documents. *JASIS*, 24:265–269.

Wee Meng Soon, Daniel Chung, Daniel Chung Yong Lim, Yong Lim, and Hwee Tou Ng. 2001. A machine learning approach to coreference resolution of noun phrases. *Computational Linguistics*, 27(4):521–544.

Simone Teufel, Advaith Siddharthan, and Dan Tidhar. 2006. Automatic classification of citation function. In *In Proceedings of EMNLP-06*.

Sandra A. Thompson and William C. Mann. 1987. Rhetorical structure theory: A framework for the analysis of texts. *Pragmatics*, 1(1):79–105.

Vladimir N. Vapnik. 1998. *Statistical Learning Theory*. Adaptive and Learning Systems for Signal Processing Communications, and control. John Wiley & Sons.

Web-Scale NLP 2008. 2008. `http://research.microsoft.com/ur/asia/research/NLP.aspx`.

M. Weinstock. 1971. Citation indexes. *Encyclopedia of Library and Information Science*, 5:16–41.

Ying Zhang, Fei Huang, and Stephan Vogel. 2005. Mining translations of oov terms from the web through. In *International Conference on Natural Language Processing and Knowledge Engineering (NLP-KE' 03)*, pages 669–670.

Author Index